Wicked San Antonio

Mike Cox

The History Press

Published by The History Press
Charleston, SC
www.historypress.com

First published 2022

Manufactured in the United States

ISBN 9781467137072

Library of Congress Control Number: 2022937931

CONTENTS

Preface

"THE WICKEDEST CITY IN THE UNION"

On December 2, 1885, nationally known evangelist Dixie Williams stepped off the train at San Antonio's International and Great Northern Railroad depot. Soon approached by a newspaper reporter, Reverend Williams said that he would be delivering a series of sermons in the Alamo City over the next few days.

He made his initial appearance that evening at the First Baptist Church and let flow with a Bible-based sermon that the *San Antonio Light* reported in fair detail the following afternoon. Near the end of the page-one article—and with no effort at transition—the reporter felt it pertinent to note that the visiting evangelist "resembles in appearance the late Ben Thompson and… is forcible and voluble in his delivery."

Given that Thompson had been a hard-drinking, thoroughly accomplished sinner who only two years earlier had been gunned down in a local saloon, some readers must have gotten a chuckle out of the reporter's comparison.

Four days later, Reverend Williams gave a sin-savaging sermon to a standing-room-only crowd at the church. This time, the preacher got a bit more specific in his remarks. Indeed, as far as many of those present that night were concerned, he had "gone from preachin' to meddlin'."

Speaking to an all-male audience, Williams declared: "San Antonio is the wickedest city in the Union, not excepting Washington—which is the wickedest outside of Hell." No God-fearing Christian countenanced sinning, but a lot of those present that night took umbrage at Williams's slander of their community.

On the other hand, the reporter said Williams's "appeal to the sympathies and the better nature of man, was feelingly dramatic and brought tears to many an eye." Well, maybe not everyone in the audience, especially after the crusader revealed that he had been "reliably informed that at least three of the prominent men of this city were constant visitors at houses of prostitution, where they regularly kept mistresses." Beyond that, he continued, there were men in the audience "who undoubtedly had only last night touched the polluted lips of a prostitute and then returned to their homes and laid their heads on the pillow by the side of their pure and trusting wives."

The reporter seemed more taken aback by how the preacher comported himself from the pulpit than at his accusations. "Such language," the unknown journalist wrote, "which was often such as is only heard in the most vulgar crowds, and seldom if ever among men who profess to be gentlemen, was never before spoken from a pulpit in San Antonio."

San Antonio probably wasn't the absolute wickedest city in the nation—New York had the Bowery, New Orleans the French Quarter and San Francisco the Barbary Coast—but it was no Salt Lake City. Residents of the Alamo City tolerated scores of cockfighting pits, around-the-clock saloons, opium dens, open prostitution and gambling joints. The presence of these venues led good people into temptation, met the needs of those already lost to their particular vice and attracted hardcases from pickpockets and con artists to robbers and killers.

Touring Texas in the early 1850s, landscape architect Frederick Law Olmsted pointed out that in San Antonio, "street affrays are numerous and characteristic." He wrote that almost every issue of the city's weekly newspaper had a fight or murder to report on. "Everybody wore guns in those days," one-time cigar store owner Sim Hart said of the Alamo City in its wild and wooly days. "It was foolish to go unarmed. The average man was all right, but there were a lot of desperadoes here in those days and they were a bad lot. You had to be prepared to take care of yourself."

Eleven years after Williams called San Antonio the nation's wickedest city, not all that much had changed in the Alamo City. "San Antonio has more saloons, bad women and gambling halls than any other city in Texas," San Antonio Christian Church pastor Bayard Craig told his congregation in a spirited sermon on January 5, 1896.

Four decades before, a visitor in 1856 described the city as "Sodom No. 2"—and they would not be the last. Beyond decrying how bad San Antonio was, periodically, elected officials cracked down on the city's

This is a staged photograph from the first decade of the twentieth century, but San Antonio has seen plenty of real gunplay over its three-hundred-plus-year history. *Postcard from author's collection.*

seedier players. And then came Prohibition. But that experiment didn't work, and well into the twentieth century, San Antonio remained a place where it was easy to get in trouble.

More than half a century after Williams's visit to and successful escape from San Antonio, a New Deal politician claimed that the Alamo City would finally be cleaned up on his watch.

In late 1939, the November 7 edition of *Look Magazine* hit the newsstands. Despite the worsening world crisis, the lead article in the magazine focused on San Antonio. If that seems unusual, given the just-begun Second World War, the content of the piece was even more unusual. "We Free a City of Vice and Crime," read the headline. The author was Maury Maverick Sr., the then-current mayor and grandson of Texas pioneer Samuel Maverick.

Before getting into how his administration had done away with vice and crime, Maverick noted that over the years, newspapers and magazines had given San Antonio "a reputation that st—...I mean smells to high heaven." Various publications, he went on, had decried the city's history of open prostitution and gambling. One publication, he said, had referred to San Antonio as the "Citadel of the Shakedown."

Finally, Maverick said, the people had enough and revolted against the corrupt "city machine."

"The worst stories that had been told about San Antonio are mild in comparison to what I really found when I took office," Maverick wrote. "I know, of course, that a mayor is supposed to be a stuffed shirt and praise the city in sweet chamber of commerce words. But I'm going to tell you the truth about San Antonio."

Maverick's truth consisted of twenty photographs and captions splashed across six pages of the magazine. The mayor said he'd already cleaned up the city's corporation court, exposed all the "shyster lawyers" who made a living off the bonds of prostitutes and gamblers, fired the police chief (who is pictured in the article with his cap pulled down over his eyes as if he were asleep, which he appears to be) and hired a new top cop, "a dam Yankee from Illinois…who knew his business and didn't have any 'friends.'"

The new chief had already cracked down on traffic law enforcement and was in the process of buying "new radio cars, lie detectors and other gadgets." Before long, the mayor claimed, "San Antonio will have the best police force in the country."

As for prostitution, Maverick admitted it was "one of our old Spanish customs" and remained a problem. "I can't stop it overnight," he wrote. However, he continued, "We don't let vice help run the town as it did before."

Alas, Maverick served only one term, and while Maverick did much to clean up the city, no elected official or police chief anywhere has ever figured a way to do away with crime. But local, state and national crime stats do vary from year to year. For instance, when the number of murders decline and stay low for a number of years, it may look like society has finally figured out how to reduce crime. And then the numbers start going up again.

While San Antonio has seen some horrific crimes and bizarre capers over its long history, so have most large U.S. cities. Still, multiple generations of Alamo City law enforcement officers have had to deal with some particularly sensational cases. So why San Antonio?

For one thing, San Antonio has always been one of Texas's largest communities, even when it was only a village with a few thousand residents. For some forty years, from the late nineteenth century until well into the twentieth century, it was the largest city in Texas. The more people a community has, the greater the odds of crime. But there are other factors to consider.

1. Remoteness: For decades, San Antonio was a distant outpost. Even after Texas began to be settled, for a long time it lay at the edge of the frontier. To the west and south were hostile Native Americans, Mexican bandits and Anglo desperadoes.

2. The military: Boys will be boys. For most of its existence, San Antonio has had a significant military presence. The U.S. Army opened a supply depot there in 1848, only three years after Texas became a state, and in 1876, it established Fort Sam Houston, which continues as an active military post. The fort and other military installations in the area provided ample customers for the city's saloons and bawdy houses well into the twentieth century.

3. Transportation crossroads: The freight and cattle trails crossing through the town brought people from elsewhere, and Mexico lay only roughly 160 miles to the south. When San Antonio gained a railroad service in 1877, even more people began passing through as the city boomed.

4. Availability of alcohol and other drugs: At one point before national Prohibition, San Antonio, as one writer put it, had more saloons than days of the year. Opiates, cocaine and marijuana added to the problem. Of course, Prohibition also fostered crime.

5. Availability of firearms: Carrying a handgun or another deadly weapon became illegal in Texas in 1871, but for a lawman to make a case, he had to see the pistol or knife. Going around with a concealed pistol was not at all uncommon in the nineteenth century and even into the early twentieth century. And while the first state gun law provided for a maximum fine of one hundred dollars for violators, there was no jail time unless an offender couldn't pay the fine and had to lay it out.

6. Finally, the quality of local law enforcement—as Mayor Maverick stressed in the late 1930s—has an impact on a city's crime statistics. Throughout its history, San Antonio has had good, bad and mediocre sheriffs, city marshals and police chiefs. At least advances in forensic science made it possible for investigators to clear cases that likely would have gone unsolved, but departmental effectiveness varied.

This book delves into San Antonio's wicked ways from its days as a small Spanish colonial settlement through modern times, though I opted to focus on a selection of notable crimes, scandals and miscellaneous examples of wickedness that occurred prior to 1970. Some are famous cases, and others are forgotten. Hopefully, you'll find all of them interesting.

But *Wicked San Antonio* is only a sampling of more than three hundred years of social history. To cover all the spectacular instances of wickedness that have taken place in the Alamo City would take a multivolume set.

1

CSI SAN ANTONIO, 1744

It's one of San Antonio's oldest recorded homicides, occurring when fewer than six hundred people lived there, but the killer's motive was timeless.

Fortunately, for history's sake, Spanish officials were first-rate bureaucrats, and despite its age, the case is well-documented in surviving official reports in the Bexar Archives, which have since been translated to English from Spanish.

Around nine o'clock on the moonlit evening of August 21, 1744, someone pounded on the door of Don Alberto Lopez, the alcalde of San Antonio de Bexar. His duties were somewhat equivalent to those of a mayor, and he also served as the village's chief law enforcement officer. After hearing what the caller had to say, the alcalde hurried to the residence of Jeronimo Flores.

There, the alcalde found a forty-eight-year-old man identified as Matias Trevino suffering from what appeared to be a bullet wound. "When I asked him who had wounded him, where and at what time, he told me that a master mason who was working in the mission of San Antonio [de Valero] had wounded him in the woods, at a distance of three-fourths of a league from this villa," Lopez later wrote in his report.

The man Trevino claimed shot him was Antonio Tello, a thirty-one-year-old stoneworker from Zacatecas who had come to Bexar in the late 1730s to oversee the building of stone structures for the missions that were then being constructed along the San Antonio River. The alcalde ordered the apprehension of "said culprit," sending a captain and four soldiers in search of the shooter. "At the same time," Lopez continued, "since there was no professional surgeon or doctor here, and since Fray Juan de los Angeles, [a priest] who is most experienced in this respect, had not come, I sent for Pedro Veserra because I had heard that he had some medical knowledge and ordered him to examine and cure [the victim's] wounds."

Meanwhile, notary and municipal council secretary Francisco de Arocha conducted a surprisingly detailed forensic investigation. Arocha noted that the victim's right wrist had been pierced by a bullet, which had caused significant nerve damage. Observing gunpowder traces on Trevino's shirt and stippling on the skin around the entrance wound, Arocha saw that the bullet had entered the right side of the man's chest and exited just below his navel, in the process tearing through Trevino's intestines. The man had also been hit on the head several times, apparently with the barrel of a firearm.

The official concluded that the contact wound was mortal and obtained a deathbed deposition from the suffering victim. Between groans, Trevino revealed what led to the shooting and how it unfolded. For some time, he had suspected that his thirty-year-old wife, Maria Rosa Guerra, was being unfaithful. Two days earlier, the man Trevino believed to be her lover, Tello, had shown up at his house. "He [Trevino]…told the said Tello that he would appreciate his not coming to his house," the notary wrote. "The said Tello did not say a word, but his [Trevino's] said wife said this to him, 'Very well; but I promise you that I shall soon be freed from these botherations, and upon my soul, I'll have you killed.'"

What further discussions Trevino and his wife had after that remark were not reported. Maybe Trevino wrote off Maria's threat as a mere angry outburst. After all, they had been married for sixteen years and had five children, a daughter and four sons. But Maria had been completely serious.

Two days later, to Trevino's surprise, Tello showed up at the unhappy couple's residence saying he had a yearling calf to give him as payment for some work Trevino had done for him. He said Trevino could pick up the meat at the corral behind the mission. After Tello left, Trevino—who intended to claim the beef—happened to tell a friend what Tello had said. "Don't be so trusting," the acquaintance cautioned, "remember what your wife said to you and that it is rumored that he has illicit relations with her. That man may kill you."

"No…he won't do that to me," Trevino replied. "Why should he kill me, when he himself told me to come for the yearling?"

Later that afternoon, Trevino rode to a wooded area behind the mission to meet Tello. There, after the calf had been killed and placed on Trevino's horse, Tello told him the carcass was slipping off. When Trevino leaned over to check, Tello produced a firearm (the reports never said whether the weapon was a handgun or rifle) and shot him. Then he started beating him on the head with the barrel of the gun, saying, "Now you'll see, cuckold."

After the shooting, Tello fled the scene. Meanwhile, Trevino managed to ride his horse to the nearby residence of his friend Jeronimo Flores. "Brother Jeronimo," Flores later said the wounded man had yelled, "confession, I have been killed, bring me a confessor." When in the process of helping Trevino from his horse, Flores asked who had shot him. The wounded man replied, "That rascal Antonio Tello, who took me to the woods under the pretext that he was going to deliver to me a calf."

Trevino died at four o'clock on the morning on August 22, and the alcalde ordered Tello's arrest for murder. When the soldiers sent to take Tello into custody returned empty-handed, they reported that Tello had sought and received refuge inside the mission.

Later that day, the priest allowed Alcalde Lopez to take a statement from Tello, who claimed he'd shot Trevino by accident, mistaking him for an Apache. Tello denied that he was having an affair with the victim's wife. Even so, Tello refused to leave the church, and the soldiers had no authority to force the issue. The alcalde returned the following day and interviewed Tello again. He continued to deny an affair with the victim's wife or any intent to kill him.

The same day, Lopez had the victim's wife arrested. He ordered the village blacksmith to place her in fetters and, since there was no jail, locked her up in a room in his house. When he took a statement from her, she denied having an affair with Tello and denied that she told Tello to kill her husband.

On August 24, not swayed by the denials of Tello and Maria, Lopez had the mission surrounded by ten soldiers and several citizens and demanded that Tello be handed over to them. But the priest told them that the murder suspect had left during the night.

Thorough as he had been in his investigation, the alcalde apparently had not anticipated that Tello would take flight. Whether the suspected killer was ever located is not known, nor is the fate of the young woman who had her husband murdered so she could take up with her lover.

What is known is that Tello's sudden departure from Bexar had an impact on the architecture of San Antonio's missions. Since Tello had already drawn up plans for the work he intended to do and since his workers had theoretically gained enough experience to finish the missions without

Spanish stonemason Antonio Tello came to the village of San Antonio de Bexar to work on Mission Alamo de Valero but fled when charged with murder. *Author's collection.*

Tello's supervision, the priests figured they did not need to bring in another master stonemason and had the workers proceed. That proved to be a bad idea. Around 1750, the roof and the upper portions of the Alamo Mission Chapel's walls collapsed as a result of shoddy post-Tello workmanship, and another master mason had to be brought to Bexar to rebuild it. But due to a lack of available manpower, the chapel was never completed and remained roofless through the 1836 siege that would make the old mission famous. In fact, nearly a century passed before the U.S. Army finally constructed a wooden roof over the historic structure in 1848. And the military added something the fugitive killer had never envisioned: the iconic hump on the chapel's façade.

2

BLOOD-SOAKED SAND

When the killing ended that summer day, more than 850 combatants lay dead on the blood-soaked sandy soil, and many of the moaning wounded would not survive.

A fierce battle won, the victorious force marched off to easily seize control of the nearby village. There, the general in charge ordered the arrest of the widows, sisters, daughters and sons of the just-defeated soldiers; he allowed his men to repeatedly rape the women and forced the victims to prepare food for his troops. Meanwhile, the women's children had to beg on the streets for food. As for the surviving male population, the general ordered the execution of ten men from the opposition every day on the public plaza, their severed heads displayed on pikes.

Did this occur somewhere in Europe during the Middle Ages?

No, this happened in and around San Antonio de Bexar in 1813. The horror of it all may be why the slaughter came to be so quickly forgotten. The Battle of the Alamo would be remembered, but the much bloodier fight known as the Battle of the Medina—the deadliest military engagement ever fought in Texas—would not. Accounts of the events of 1813 can of course be found, but there have been only a few books written about it and no movies with spin-off products like comic books, toy rifles, coonskin caps and, not to mention, Alamo snow globes and T-shirts.

When comparing the Battle of Media to the fall of the Alamo twenty-three years later, the only similarity is that both events were related to putting down a revolution.

Reenactors in the type of uniforms that would have been worn by the Spanish soldiers at the Battle of Medina. *Author's collection.*

For more than 120 years, the province that would become Texas had been part of Spain's New World empire, a buffer between the other provinces and French-controlled Louisiana. But in September 1810, separatists launched a revolt against the Spanish crown, the beginning of a long revolution that culminated in 1821 with the creation of the Republic of Mexico.

While many New World descendants of the Spanish conquerers and people of mixed blood wanted freedom from Spain, firebrands in the young United States also had their eyes on Texas.

To that end, a rebel force commanded by José Bernardo Gutiérrez de Lara and U.S. Army lieutenant Augustus William Magee invaded Spanish Texas in the summer of 1812. Marching under an emerald flag, they hoped to wrest the province from Spain and create their own country. They called themselves the Republican Army of the North. As for Magee, he died of disease that fall, but the revolution lived on.

On March 29, 1813, the invaders defeated Spanish royalists in what came to be called the Battle of Rosillo. Having taken over Bexar, the rebels—who converged on the village plaza carrying the severed heads of some of the royalists—soon executed the province's governor along with more than a dozen prisoners they had taken in the fight. Barely a week after the battle, the victors adopted a declaration of independence on April 6.

Early that August, a Cuban-born revolutionary named José Álvarez de Toledo y DuBois deposed Gutiérrez and took control of the new republic. The brutality of the short-lived revolution was over the top for some of the American filibusters who had taken part in the fight, but most of the residents of Bexar accepted the carnage as the price of freedom from European control. Naturally enough, the Spanish Crown didn't see it that way.

With orders to retake Bexar and crush the new republic, General Joaquín de Arrendondo, commandant of Spain's eastern interior provinces, led a force of more than 1,800 Spanish regulars north from Laredo to put down the revolt.

Early that August, rebel scouts spotted Arrendondo's army fording the Frio River roughly fifty miles south of Bexar. Most of the Americans who had participated in the revolution's initial fighting argued that they should dig in and wait until the Spanish troops arrived outside the town. Had their thinking prevailed, an Alamo-like siege might have taken place. But the majority of the revolutionaries wanted to carry the fight to the Spanish, hopefully sparing their families and the town from experiencing the ravages of war.

On August 15, a rebel army of roughly 1,400 composed of Tejanos (as those of Hispanic descent born in the province were known), American filibusters, Spanish army deserters and Native American allies marched from Bexar to the strains of martial music and the cheers of local women and other noncombatants.

The Republican Army of the North hoped to stage a surprise attack on the Spanish regulars, but when the rebels encountered a royalist scouting party on the morning of August 18, they opened fire and gave away their presence. Later that day, under a blistering summer sun, the rebels charged uphill toward Arrendondo's fortified position. But their advance was slowed by the deep, sandy soil they had to cross, making the rebels easy targets for the Spaniards. Still, neither side prevailed until around 4:00 p.m., when, following a pause in the fighting, the royalists regrouped and forced the rebels into an unorganized retreat that quickly evolved into a massacre. Losing only 55 of their own, the royalists killed more than 850 of the rebels and captured the survivors.

Arrendondo took time to bury his casualties but left the hundreds of slain rebels lying where they fell to rot in the heat. Meanwhile, General Toledo had managed to escape death and left the province hoping to organize another invasion. (He did so in 1814, but it was not successful.)

Known as La Quinta, this adobe, following the Battle of Medina, was packed with more than three hundred female prisoners who were subjected to rape and forced labor. Eighteen of the women died from suffocation. *Author's collection.*

Historian Robert Thonhoff has noted that the battle and the period of vengeance that followed cut the total population of the province of Texas (estimated at roughly 4,500) by roughly one-third. Of the adult male population, more than half were killed.

Despite the battle's terrible toll, exactly where it occurred has never been determined. A dozen locations are considered possible sites, but the search for definitive archaeological evidence continues. Three historical markers in either southern Bexar or northern Atascosa Counties purport to denote the site, but none of them has been confirmed by archaeologists.

While the venue of the battle remains a mystery, the documented history of the battle includes this fact: in his official report of the battle, General Arredondo singled out three officers who "conducted themselves with great bravery" that day. One of them was a nineteen-year-old lieutenant the general identified as "Don Antonio Santa Anna." Twenty years later, as a general in command of his own army, Santa Anna would return to San Antonio.

3

SANTA ANNA'S NOT-SO-ORIGINAL SIN

If the tale told by a former Mexican army sergeant who took part in the storming of the Alamo is true, General Antonio Lopez de Santa Anna had more than military tactics on his mind when he marched his troops into San Antonio de Bexar that winter day of 1836.

When, thirteen days later, Santa Anna carried out his declaration that all the independence-minded foreigners occupying the old Spanish mission would be shown no quarter, the slaughter amounted to a war crime. Beyond that, while laying siege to the Alamo, the president of the Republic of Mexico committed what under modern Texas law would be considered first-degree rape by deception, not to mention sacrilege under the Roman Catholic Church. But the authoritarian general's alleged sexual escapade would not be revealed for decades, at least not in Texas.

The disclosure of Santa Anna's purported perfidy—which has a definite ring of truth—came in Austin, some eighty miles north of San Antonio, when former Texas Ranger captain John S. "Rip" Ford told the story to a small audience at the capital city's nascent public library on the blustery fall night of November 5, 1875.

As the *Austin Daily Statesman* reported two days later: "Those present were highly entertained by Col. John S. Ford, member of the Constitutional Convention [then meeting in the capital city], who gave some interesting and new reminiscences of the Battle of the Alamo, which information he had gained from a soldier of the Mexican army, now a resident and policeman of Brownsville, on the Rio Grande frontier."

Unfortunately for the newspaper's readers, the article did not reveal what the "interesting and new reminiscences" were, nor did it give the name of Ford's informant. That would not come for nearly six more years, when Ford published an account of Francisco Becerra's experiences at the Alamo, including the ruse he claimed Santa Anna employed to have his way with a seventeen-year-old señorita.

Filling four tabloid-size newspaper pages, Becerra's recollections, which Ford styled "A Mexican Sergeant's Recollections of the Alamo & San Jacinto," appeared in the April 1882 edition of the *Texas Mute Ranger*. This was the student publication of the State Deaf and Dumb Asylum (as it was then called). Ford served as the institution's director. Even then, Becerra's story did not generate any additional news media attention. In fact, the as-told-to narrative went largely forgotten for another sixty-plus years.

Most of Becerra's recollections deal with the Alamo siege and the rout that Santa Anna's army followed on April 21 at San Jacinto. In between is a story Ford labeled "The Incident."

Early in the siege, Becerra began, a detachment under the command of General Manuel Fernandez Castrillon began confiscating timber for use in the construction of several bridges across the San Antonio River. The soldiers were stripping the wood from residences that had been hastily vacated with the approach of the Mexican force. At one house, however, the soldiers found a Mexican woman and her daughter. "The girl was beautiful," Becerra said. "The general asked the mother what she was doing there and if she was not afraid. She told him it was her home, and she had no other place to go, that she was not afraid. She was well bred and intelligent, though poorly clad."

Back at Santa Anna's headquarters, Castrillon told the president about the lady and her lovely daughter. At that, Becerra went on, "Santa Anna was in a great fever to see the pretty girl. He told Castrillon that he wanted her and asked him to carry a message to her mother." Clearly an officer and a gentleman, Castrillon said he would willingly abide by any order from the president and commander in chief, but "in that particular case, he begged to be excused and requested the president to employ someone else."

Colonel Jose Vicente Minon (Becerra mistakenly refers to him as a general) did not share his immediate superior's reluctance to do the president's bidding, so he went to the woman to report that Santa Anna would take great pleasure in becoming acquainted with her daughter. Of course, the mother readily understood that Santa Anna had more than a casual meet and greet in mind. Again, Ford-Becerra said, "She replied that she was a respectable lady of good family and had always conducted herself with propriety; that her deceased

Right: General Antonio Lopez de Santa Anna took the Alamo by force and a young wife by deceit. *Author's collection.*

Below: No images of Santa Anna's bride are known to exist, but this vintage drawing shows how Mexican señoritas dressed in the mid-1830s. *Author's collection.*

husband was an honorable man and commanded a company in the Mexican service; that President Santa Anna was not her president and could not get her daughter except by marriage. She was not only inflexible, but defiant."

Minon returned to relay the disappointing news. Admitting that he had failed to convince the lady to turn her daughter over to His Excellency, he said that he had a man in his command "who was well educated, a great rascal and capable of performing all sorts of tricks, even the personating of a priest." Clearly, the officer understood what would come to be called the "bring me solutions, not problems" management principle.

The forty-two-year-old president, having batched it for some five weeks on the march from the Mexican interior to the rebellious province, told Minon to summon this soldier. Cheerfully agreeing to help His Excellency with a different sort of military conquest, the man found a real priest and told him that the president of his country requested the proper raiment and religious paraphernalia to perform a marriage ceremony.

Since arranged marriages were quite common in Mexico at the time, the mother of the teenager consented to her daughter's marriage. After all, the groom-to-be was the president of the Republic of Mexico, even if she didn't support him politically. What the soon-to-be bride thought of her sudden engagement was not reported. In fact, Becerra did not even mention her name in his account.

Ford's retelling of Becerra's story had long since been forgotten when Southern Methodist University professor Lon Tinkle, who also worked as book editor for the *Dallas Morning News*, began researching the Alamo. At the University of Texas, he found Ford's retelling of Becerra's story and used it in his 1958 book on the siege, *Thirteen Days to Glory*. Another twenty-two years went by before Texana dealer John H. Jenkins published Becerra's account as a small hardback book with an introduction by Corpus Christi historian Dan Kilgore.

Historians believe Santa Anna's "wife" may have been Melchora Inlega Barerra. Indeed, a teenager by that name whose father had served as a Mexican Army officer did live in San Antonio with her widowed mother in 1836. And she apparently was quite a looker. "[T]he little girls of our town, I do assure you, find themselves tolerably well attended to, and they do not appear much displeased at some attention being shown to them," John W. Smith wrote to Thomas Jefferson Chambers from San Antonio on September 2, 1835. He said he'd seen a young lady he called "Melchorcite" (a misspelling of "Melchorcita") with her mother at a fandango and that she was "fine as a fiddle."

No matter the name of the blushing bride, the fake wedding before a phony priest took place at el presidente's quarters in late February. "The honeymoon," Ford quoted Becerra, "lasted until the army marched for the Guadalupe [River]," a little over three weeks after the Mexican forces overran the Alamo and killed its roughly two hundred defenders. Becerra claimed to have done some of the killing that day.

When Santa Anna bid his bride adieu, he sent her in Colonel Minon's carriage to San Luis Potosi to be "placed in the care of a very respectable family." Before long, it became evident that the faux first lady (who, since Santa Anna was already married, was actually the second lady) was pregnant. "In due course…she became the mother of a son," Becerra told Ford.

As with many things connected to the Alamo story, there are variant accounts of "The Incident."

Manuel Villa-Amor, who wrote a book about Santa Anna that was published in Mexico in 1857, said that the bogus nuptials occurred after the siege, though that does not seem likely. Villa-Amor further maintained in his *Biografio del General Santa Anna* that the president immediately sent his new significant other south to Mexico City, which seems even less likely given the general's well-known penchant for womanizing. Santa Anna's early biographer also didn't seem to see the duped soldier's daughter as all that wicked. Santa Anna's early biographer concluded: "The virtuous *bejarena* [female inhabitant of San Antonio de Bejar, later more commonly spelled Bexar]…believes…she is the *presidenta* of the Republic, and thus loses that very virginity she had defended with such honor."

More than a century later, in his *Santa Anna: The Story of an Enigma Who Once Was Mexico* (1964), author W.H. Calcott said the young woman had been "duly installed as mistress in a very good dwelling just a few doors from the public square of Jalapa, where legend still has it that she lived, childless, for many years."

Whatever else the circumstances, no one who has written of "The Incident" has challenged that the wedding was fake and the "marriage" a sex crime.

4

DARK SIDE OF THE ALAMO

Three Alamo-related expressions are almost universally known: "A line in the sand," "Remember the Alamo" and "The Alamo had no back door."

The world will never know, as legend holds, whether Colonel William B. Travis used his saber to draw a line on the ground and invited all who chose to fight to the death to cross it. But the expression endures as resolutely as our collective memory of the siege that ended on the morning of March 6, 1836.

The second leg of the triad, "Remember the Alamo," is well-documented as the last three words hundreds of Mexican soldiers heard before they died at the hands of Sam Houston's vengeful army during the Battle of San Jacinto on April 21, 1836.

But who first noted that the old Spanish mission in San Antonio had no back door? And what if the Alamo did have a back door—or at least a secret escape route?

On September 15, 1894, the *Eagle Pass Guide* reprinted a story from the *St. Louis Globe-Democrat*, "The Alamo's Secret Passage." The piece began: "There has been a tradition among the Mexicans of this city [San Antonio], since the early part of the present century, that the old Alamo and Conception Missions are connected…by means of an underground passage, and a discovery has just been made…which leads to the belief that the tradition is well founded." A few days earlier, the story went, workmen who were digging a well on the farm of one Walter Scott, just south of town, struck a layer of rock. "After penetrating this barrier, they came upon a passage which is about eight feet in height and five feet wide," the story continued.

> *The sides are walled with rock slabs, and the bottom seems to be laid with a material resembling cement. The passage runs in a north and south direction, and at the time the discovery was made, it was half filled with water, it being just after heavy rains.... The top of the passage is about twelve feet from the surface. It is in direct line between the two missions, and Mr. Scott is thoroughly convinced that he has at last discovered the long-lost passage, and that upon further exploration, he will bring some wonderful things to light.*

The article said a brief exploration of the passage had been made, but no one had gone very far because of the water. The unidentified author offered that secret passages were common in the missions of Mexico and the Southwest and that they were "constantly [being] discovered and explored, even at this late day, and in some of them, immense amounts of treasure have been brought to light."

No, the Alamo didn't have a back door or secret tunnel. *Author's collection.*

While that's possible, the notion of secret tunnels is a definite folktale subcategory, often connected with the broader treasure story genre. The idea behind the tunnels, of course, is that they were used as escape routes in the event of Native American attack.

The story went on:

> *When the Franciscan fathers came to the new world, they found many enemies…with which to contend in their work of advancing Catholicism and civilization. They built these missions and fortified them so that in case of attack from the savages or other…enemies they could make resistance.* [It]…*is a well-known fact that in many places in Mexico, they were successfully used in turbulent times, and when the attacking party would enter the religious edifice, it would be found deserted.*

The passages were both well-built and well-disguised, the story noted.

"Another thing that lends color to the theory that the Alamo and Conception Missions are connected," the story said, "is that in the north wing of the Alamo in one of the cell-like rooms that was formerly occupied by the severe and sober-appearing monks, there is a spot about five feet square in the cement floor which within the past few years has sunk several inches, and when one walks upon the spot, there is a hollow sound."

Should the existence of a passage running three miles from the Alamo to Mission Conception be proven, the story said, "the discovery will also reveal that the Texas martyrs who lost their lives in the Alamo, had they known of the existence of this outlet, [could] have saved their lives by escaping through it."

None of the basic Alamo histories mention anything about a tunnel having ever been found, though scholars do believe some of the Alamo defenders tried to escape once they realized they had no hope of survival inside the mission. The underground rock-lined structure found in 1894, assuming the story wasn't made up, might have been a remnant of the Spanish irrigation system that connected the Alamo to the San Antonio River.

As for the "back door" line, it is variously attributed to the late Maury Maverick Jr. or some unnamed member of the Daughters of the Republic of Texas. Supposedly, when President John F. Kennedy visited the Alamo in 1960, he asked that following his appearance, he be escorted out the back door of the old mission. "There is no back door to the Alamo," Kennedy learned. "That's why they were all heroes."

Indeed, history has been kind to the men who died in the Alamo, affording them immortality as martyred heroes. The names of many of these men are carved in stone on the Alamo monument in downtown San Antonio. Some who fell that Sunday morning did not get listed on the granite cenotaph, though subsequent research has assured their place in history as an "Alamo defender," two words that stand strong in the collective consciousness of Texans. But for an altogether different reason, seven other men deserve scrutiny.

A little-known letter from Colonel Travis, written early in the morning on January 28, 1836, provides the sketchy details of a less noble story. From his camp at Burnam's Crossing on the Colorado River (present La Grange), the twenty-six-year-old lieutenant colonel penned a private letter to Texas's provisional governor, Henry Smith.

As soon as Colonel Travis dispatched his report, he broke camp and resumed his "march to the relief of Bexar." With thirty men, Travis was on his way to bolster the Texas garrison at San Antonio, which General Antonio Lopez de Santa Anna was expected to attempt to retake when he arrived from the interior. "Our affairs are gloomy indeed," Travis wrote. "The people are cold and indifferent. They are worn down and exhausted with war, and in consequence of dissensions between contending and rival chieftains, they have lost all confidence in their own government and officers."

The revolution had started the previous October with the seizure of a cannon at Gonzales. Two months later, Texans had taken San Antonio from the Mexican army, sending General Martín Perfecto de Cos in disgraceful retreat toward the Rio Grande. Since that December 1835 victory, many of the Texas soldiers, all volunteers, had gone home. "The patriotism of a few has done much," Travis wrote, "but that is becoming worn down." Unless the government raised enough money to fund a strong regular army and began drafting men to serve in the militia, he continued, "war cannot be carried on in Texas."

Indeed, Texans seemed to have lost their appetite for independence. Also, what modern military strategists call "command and control" was anemic at best. Travis certainly was giving the cause his best efforts. He had used his personal credit to obtain horses and equipment and had "neither slept day nor night" since receiving orders to join the Texas garrison at San Antonio.

Not only was Travis astute in his assessment of conditions in Texas, but in his letter, the young officer also seems to have been prescient. He had no enthusiasm for his assignment but wrote, "I shall however go on and do my duty; if I am sacrificed, unless I receive new orders." A modern writer would have said "EVEN if I am sacrificed," but that is clearly what Travis meant.

Some of his men may have had the same premonition. For whatever reason, Travis listed nine men as having deserted his command since he left San Felipe for San Antonio. Those nine men could not have saved the Alamo, but they most assuredly would have died there had they not gone AWOL. Travis's list, as compiled by his sergeant:

- White (No first name given.)
- John Cole
- Baker (No first name given.)
- Andrew Smith
- Ginnings (The sergeant surely meant to spell Jennings. No first name given.)
- William Smith
- Solomon Bardwell
- Alfonso Steele
- Wiley (No first name given.)

Baker, Andrew Smith and Ginnings/Jennings also made off with government-owned horses. In addition, Smith took a saddle, bridle, blanket, rifle and shot pouch owned by the military.

How these men reacted when they heard that the Alamo had fallen with every defender killed is better left to the imagination. Maybe they praised God that they had chosen to chicken out. Perhaps they felt a crushing guilt, a survivor's reaction that psychologists today say is common.

In fairness, Travis's list constitutes little more than an indictment. Record keeping back then left much to be desired, as the use of four incomplete names suggests. Historians need to do more work before these men can be written off with certainty as cowards.

At least two of the men on the list did redeem themselves. Both Bardwell and Steele rejoined the army and fought under Sam Houston at San Jacinto, the April 21, 1836 battle that assured Texas's independence. Steele took a Mexican musket ball in the fight but recovered. Later, he set down his recollections of the battle, an important contribution to Texas history. But nowhere in his memoir does he own up to deserting Travis on the way to the Alamo.

5

"I AIM FOR YOUR HEART"

San Antonio would grow into a charming city with numerous popular tourist attractions, but back in the days of the Republic of Texas, merely passing through town could be dangerous to one's health.

The spring of 1840 offers a couple of cases in point.

Earlier that year, a small party of Comanches rode into town. They told Henry Karnes, the ranking military commander, that they were interested in making peace. Karnes said that if they wanted to talk about getting along, they needed to return with all the Texans they were known to have captured.

Sixty-five Native Americans showed up on March 19. The various chiefs went inside the old Spanish government building Casa Reales to meet with two commissioners appointed by President Mirabeau B. Lamar. Also on hand was Colonel William S. Fisher and two companies of soldiers. The Texas officials had a peace treaty ready for signing, but the Comanches had brought only one prisoner with them, a fifteen-year-old named Matilda Lockhart. The Comanches said she was the only prisoner they had. Any others, they continued, were in the possession of other bands, a matter outside of their control. In response to that, the representatives of the republic said the government would hold the chiefs as hostages until the other captives were returned.

When one of the chiefs bolted for the door and stabbed one of the soldiers who tried to block his way, on Fisher's order, the troops who had been standing in the room opened fire on the Native Americans. When the black powder gun smoke cleared, thirty-eight Native Americans lay dead along with seven Texans. But several dozen violent deaths in a few minutes' time was not the end of the story.

The Comanches, understandably, were outraged at what they saw as a betrayal. Within a couple of weeks, after word of the massacre spread, an even larger contingent of Native Americans came to town. Soldiers stood guard as Chief Isimanica and his warriors threatened the town. Mary A. Maverick described the scene in her diary:

> *Chief Isimanica with another warrior rode daringly into the public square and circled around it, then rode some distance down Commerce Street and back, shouting all the while, offering fight and heaping abuse and insults upon the Americans. Isimanica was in full war paint and almost naked. He stopped longest at Black's saloon, at the northeast corner of the square; he shouted defiance, he rose in his stirrups, shook his clenched fist, raved and foamed at the mouth.*

Someone communicated to the chief that if he and his people wanted a fight, Texas troops camped near the old San Jose Mission would give them one. Hearing that, the chief and his warriors rode to the military encampment.

However, Captain William Redd, the officer in charge, opted for watchful waiting, not more shooting. The town's mayor, Lysander Wells, did not like Redd's handling of the situation. He saw the situation as an opportunity to further reduce the Comanche population. Wells's credentials supported that "kill 'em all and let God sort 'em out" attitude. He had fought in the Battle of San Jacinto and had killed quite a few of the Comanches in the late unpleasantness in the government building. In October 1838, he was indicted for assaulting a San Antonio doctor over a political disagreement. Less is known of Redd, who had recently returned to Texas from his native Alabama.

One thing that was common knowledge at the time, however, was that Redd had scandalously arrived in San Antonio with a young woman who was not his wife. In an attempt to disguise that fact, she was wearing male attire when they arrived in town. That is what led Wells to accuse the captain of operating a "petticoat government." Redd was duly insulted, but it was Wells who challenged the captain to a duel. Of course, Redd readily accepted. Honor would be resolved.

The two men met soon thereafter at 6:00 a.m. where the Ursuline Academy would later be built. "I aim for your heart," Redd said as they leveled pistols at each other. "And I aim for your brains," Wells countered.

When both gentleman "win" a duel, it's time for a couple of funerals. *Author's collection.*

When the pistols went off, as Mary Maverick described it, "Redd sprang high into the air and fell dead with a bullet in his brain." Wells, true to his adversary's claim, had been shot in the heart but lived.

Someone found a freshly issued marriage license in Redd's coat pocket. He had been planning to marry the woman he'd brought to Texas from Alabama.

Mayor Wells lingered for two weeks, begging that someone shoot him to put him out of his misery or bring him a pistol so he could do it himself. No one was inclined to help him either way.

The duel and the difference of opinion that led to it left many of Wells's soldiers at odds with Redd's men. Higher-ups in the republic's military viewed the situation as something more serious. As the *Austin Gazette* reported, "An express arrived in town Monday last…bringing intelligence of the death of two of the bravest officers in the Texian service and a mutiny among the regular troops." Troops were sent from the capital city to San Antonio to calm things down, which their presence succeeded in doing.

Of the two dead duelists, Mary Maverick concluded, "These men were both brave and tried soldiers! What a sad ending to their young and promising lives."

6
"LASHES WELL LAID ON..."

Texas's time as an independent republic is often portrayed as a period of near lawlessness with scoundrels of every stripe, from swindlers and horse thieves to killers, all swarming the new nation like so many cockroaches. But "lawlessness" did not mean Texas lacked a body of criminal statutes, just that with little organized law enforcement and plenty of open country to hide out in, there was a lot of crime.

For wrongdoers unlucky enough to be arrested, charged and found guilty of a felony, the laws of the Republic of Texas seem almost medieval in comparison to twenty-first-century criminal codes. During the days of the republic, for instance, brutal corporal punishment was meted out for offenses that seem trivial today. Theft under twenty dollars, though that was a lot of money in the 1830s and '40s, was punishable by a fine of thirty-nine-plus lashes "well laid on." Floggings were administered in public, the criminal tied to a whipping post.

A San Antonio woman named Encarnacion Pulido, for instance, was convicted of possessing two pair of shoes that belonged to one William B. Jacques. They were valued at $5.50. Following her trial, she was bound to the public whipping post, which stood on the south side of Casa Real (now known as the Spanish Governor's Palace), and given the full number of lashes on her bare back.

Court records from this early period are sketchy, but what official verbiage that survives points to the case against Pulido as being more involved than merely stealing footwear. The shoes were taken in what was described as "the

During the days of the Republic of Texas, even some minor breaches of the law were punishable by public flogging. *Author's collection.*

robbery of several carts of merchandise belonging to [Jacques]." Whether *robbery* meant the carts had been waylaid and their drivers forced to give up their goods or be injured or killed or was incorrectly used as a synonym for *burglary* is not known, but one of the suspects soon had the opportunity to sincerely regret not having told authorities the truth about the matter.

One Veneclado Pacheco swore before a justice of the peace that he had purchased the goods in question on December 10, 1838. When that was proven to be a lie, he was convicted of perjury. For that offense, Judge James W. Robinson sentenced him to receive fifty lashes.

Though public flogging was intended as a painful way to inspire criminals to better behavior in the future, the disfiguring punishment could result in lasting nerve damage, death from shock or infection.

Along the frontier, stealing a man's horse was a serious crime. The laws of the republic set the punishment as a fine, thirty-nine lashes and the branding of the letter "T" (for thief) on the convicted person's hand.

On October 16, 1839, the Bexar County Grand Jury indicted Juan Galvan for horse theft. The following day, the defendant asked that San Antonio pioneer Samuel A. Maverick represent him in court. Maverick had read the law and surely successfully defended many of his clients, but that would not be the case for Galvan. A jury, on October 22, found him guilty of "stealing a bay mare belonging to Jose Antonio Navara" but recommended that the defendant be shown the mercy of the court. Sparing Galvan the angst and indignity of undergoing a public whipping and branding, the judge sentenced him to hang.

That magistrate's exercise of judicial discretion aside, the Republic of Texas's statutes provided the death penalty for murder, rape, robbery, burglary, arson and counterfeiting. A congressional act in 1840 eliminated hanging as a penalty for counterfeiting, but conviction remained punishable by a fine and up to thirty-nine lashes.

By the time Texas became a state in 1845, lashing in the United States was beginning to fall out of favor, as it was seen as "cruel and unusual" punishment. In the new state's first set of criminal statutes, lashing was eliminated as a punishment (excepting for enslaved people), and the practice continued to decline elsewhere in the United States.

7
RIVER NYMPHS

The San Antonio River is not the stream it once was.

The following is how visitor George W. Bonnell described it in 1840: "The [river] is formed by about one hundred large springs in a beautiful valley four miles above the city. Many of these springs would singly form a river; and when they unite in San Antonio, they formed a bold and rapid stream of two hundred feet in width and about four feet deep over the shoals."

For generations, the river that attracted Spanish missionaries in the late seventeenth century ran strong, its waters clear blue and cool. "The temperature of the water is the same throughout the year," wrote another visitor in 1843, "neither too warm nor too cold for bathing, and not a single day passes with the inhabitants indulging in the favourite and healthy exercise of swimming, which is practiced by everybody, from morning till evening; and the traveler along the shores of this beautiful river will constantly see hundreds of children, of all ages and colour, swimming and diving like so many ducks."

It's true that Bexarinos dumped their waste and washed their clothes and bodies in the river, but they knew the flow of the everlasting springs would wash the dirt and grime downstream to the Gulf of Mexico. And just as no sane or sober person today would take a shower wearing clothes, early San Antonio residents bathed nude in the river without shame. No one thought anything of this perfectly sensible pursuit of good hygiene until Texas violently separated itself from the Republic of Mexico in 1836 and

When San Antonio banned nude bathing in the river, floating bathhouses were popular for a time. *Author's collection.*

the number of Anglos either moving to or visiting the newly independent nation began to increase.

Immigrants and travelers who were used to bathing in private were surprised at the casual manner in which men and women bathed naked and innocently cavorted in the river—not that men far from home took offense at seeing young ladies enjoying themselves in the river.

While traveling around Texas in the mid-1840s, German Dr. Ferdinand von Roemer observed:

> *It was quite a startling spectacle to see here just above the bridge in the heart of the city a number of Mexican women and girls bathing entirely naked. Unconcerned about our presence, they continued their exercises while laughing and chattering, showing themselves perfect masters of the art of swimming. Several times, a few of them were carried near us by the stream, and they would dive and reappear again quite a distance below the bridge. If this was done to hide themselves from our view, it was the wrong thing to do, for the water* [was] *so clear, one could see the smallest pebble at the bottom.*

As word spread across Texas and the nation that nude women could regularly be seen freely frolicking in the river, San Antonio gained one of its earliest tourist attractions. "From early evening till the hour of midnight, the inhabitants flock to [the river] in crowds for the purpose of bathing, and then the forms of hundreds of young and beautiful nymphs may be seen joyfully gamboling amongst its lipid waves," wrote one-time visitor John Frost in his *Perilous Adventures By Land and Sea*. "It is by no means an unusual sight to behold the forms of three or four young brunettes come dashing down the current, with their dark hair floating over their shoulders and gliding like dolphins in the sea."

Frost's book came out in 1884, but the visit to Texas that inspired his fond recollection of the river nymphs had occurred in the early to mid-1840s. While decades had passed, his experiences in San Antonio clearly remained vivid:

> *As I stood gazing on the various forms before me, I beheld one younger and more delicate, rolling, curvetting, and sporting among the waves, whose tapering limbs and well-formed figure alone amidst the sparkling waters* [was] *like alabaster when exposed to the sunlight....Her flaxen ringlets fell wantonly about her white neck and half-developed bosom. She seemed artless and sinless as a child of the coral caves of the deep, deep ocean—but when her full blue eyes turned up, and its glance met, in wild surprise, with ours, a blush of modest consciousness passed over her check, when she darted to the bottom to rise no more till distance had deprived us of the powers of discrimination.*

But as the prim and proper Victorian mindset began to become the norm, what early visitors like Frost had enjoyed watching more commonly came to be viewed as indecent. In an era when it was considered racy for a woman to expose an ankle, such licentious behavior had to stop.

By the 1850s, the city's governing body made nude bathing in the river and along San Pedro Creek illegal. However, the city could not control what happened beyond the city limits, so Bexar County's rural residents got a bye on riverine nudity for a while longer.

The January 15, 1859 edition of *Frank Leslie's Illustrated Newspaper*, the *USA Today* of its time, featured a fanciful engraving of a group of bare-breasted women and their children bathing beneath a willow tree on the river's edge. "Primitive Bathing, Near San Antonio—From a Sketch by Our Correspondent," read the caption.

This engraving of women cavorting in the San Antonio River appeared across the nation in *Frank Leslie's Illustrated Newspaper. Author's collection.*

To get around the new city ordinance, private and for-rent bathhouses sprang up along the river like so many water lilies.

On April 7, 1855, a woman identified in newspaper ads only as "Mad Masse" announced that at considerable expense, she had "erected and fitted a spacious bathhouse" on her riverfront property and would be offering hot and cold baths to "ladies and gentlemen of the city." From sunup to noon, the baths were available to ladies only. Male customers got the evening shift. Season tickets were available, "the terms of which could be learned by personal application." "As it is a well-established fact that bathing is conducive to health, it is unnecessary for us to commend Mad Masse's Bath House," the *San Antonio Herald* declared. "It is sufficient to announce there is such a place to secure it a liberal patronage." Mad Masse sold her business less than two weeks later, but the new owner kept it open.

Another nationally published engraving, this one in the October 1879 issue of *Harper's New Monthly*, showed a couple of wooden bathhouses extending into the river directly behind someone's residence or public accommodation. "These bathhouses were usually around ten feet square and were enclosed with gunny sacks nailed on wooden frames, after which they were given a coat of whitewash to produce a beautiful effect in contrast to the clear blue water of the river," Alamo City old-timer Fred Mosebach wrote in the *San*

Antonio Express in the early 1930s. He continued, "As a means of buoyancy, the bathhouses rested on empty barrels, closed on both ends to render them airtight. As the river was from eight to ten, twelve and even fifteen feet deep at these points, the bathhouses were provided with wooden floors, which could be raised or lowered according to the depth of water desired."

Whether anything other than bathing ever occurred in any of those floating bathrooms, Mosebach did not mention. He did, however, note that the river had seen much romance and tragedy. "On its placid waters, there has been many a boat ride as an interesting prelude to a happy romance," he wrote, "and it likewise proved a watery grave when a romance was shattered after a roseate dream to awakening on the stern realities of life and its meaning, or somebody rocked the boat." Whether he meant "rocked the boat" literally or figuratively is open to interpretation.

Old customs are not easily washed away. As late as 1899, city fathers felt it necessary to revise two earlier ordinances dealing with river bathing. The revision to chapter 5, section 1, page 176 stated:

> *All persons are expressly forbidden to bathe or swim in San Antonio River, or in the San Pedro Creek, after 5 o'clock a.m., and before 8 p.m. Also, at any time to bathe in an un-becoming manner, or to remain naked on the riverbank in sight of those passing by or residing near the same, under a penalty, in either case, of not less than two dollars ($2.00) nor more than five dollars ($5.00). Should the person convicted fail to pay such fine, he shall be committed to jail for not less than two days nor more than five days.*

The other ordinance (Revised Criminal Ordinances, 1899, chapter 44; section 14) had to do with bathhouse construction, again indicating that despite the city's water and wastewater system, the tradition continued to at least some extent. "All bathhouses now or hereafter to be constructed in the river shall, from and after the passage of this ordinance, be so arranged only as to rise with and on the water in case of flood."

Floods or no floods, as San Antonio continued to urbanize, the advent of a water and sewage system pulled the proverbial plug on river bathing.

8

FOR WHOM THE BELL TOLLED

Every night at ten o'clock, the city marshal or one of his deputies rang the city bell. Fifteen minutes later, the bell tolled again. San Antonio residents or visitors could set their watches by the daily bells, but as comforting as it may have been to most people, the ringing of the bell was not intended as a public service—it was a warning to enslaved people.

When the city bell first tolled each night, unaccompanied enslaved people had fifteen minutes to get off the streets, or they would be going to jail unless they carried a written pass from their owner. But even a pass was only good for one night. Once in the city's custody, an enslaved person found violating the curfew remained in jail until their "master, mistress, employer or person having custody and charge of such slave" came to claim them. First, however, the owner had to pay the city a $2.50 fee to cover "all costs of arrest, commitment, notice and liberation."

Totaling more than 1,900 words and containing 21 sections, the city statute was styled, "An Ordinance—To Regulate the Conduct of Slaves and Free Persons of Color in the City of San Antonio." City aldermen approved it on August 25, 1860, and it went into effect immediately.

Beyond requiring that enslaved people were off the streets by 10:15 p.m. (9:15 p.m. from October 1 to April 1), the ordinance barred certain activities on the part of the enslaved or free Black people. Since enslaved people had no legal rights, the measure regulated them by providing penalties for white people who allowed certain behaviors. For instance, the proprietor of any saloon or store that sold intoxicating liquors or drink was subject to a fine

Before the Civil War, Bexar County fielded slave patrols to arrest Black Americans found out at night without a pass. *Author's collection.*

of five dollars to fifty dollars if caught allowing the enslaved to congregate on his or her premises. It also was illegal for a white proprietor to permit the enslaved to play cards or engage in any other form of gambling while on their premises. Any enslaved person found gaming could receive up to twenty lashes.

The ordinance also prohibited the enslaved from renting a room, house "or tenement" that was separate from their owner's property. Any white person renting property to an enslaved person could be fined up to fifty dollars.

Owners could not allow their enslaved hands to work for money; the enslaved could not sell any produce or other article without the consent of their owner; and the enslaved could not "go at large and trade as a free person." The penalty for that was up to thirty-nine lashes. The ordinance also prohibited an enslaved person's possession of a firearm, gunpowder, sword, bowie knife or other deadly weapon. Any enslaved person caught with a weapon was subject to a maximum of thirty-nine lashes.

Other sections of the ordinance barred more than five enslaved people from gathering in public, "unless it be for religious worship," but even then, they could not gather without "the presence of at least one respectable slaveholder." One exception to this was a ball, or dance, that was held for enslaved people. But such an event had to have a permit from the city.

The ordinance did not speak directly to the matter of runaway enslaved people, which was covered by state law. The *San Antonio Ledger* of March 15, 1856, gave the details of one striking case involving a fugitive enslaved person.

On March 2, on the road to Castroville, San Antonio resident Frank Schulter passed two riders who caught his eye. One was a man who looked to be about sixty years old; the other was a mixed-race boy in his teens. Both riders were armed. At the time, Schulter didn't think too much about it, but when he got to town, he happened to notice an advertisement offering an award for a runaway "mulatto." Remembering the boy he'd seen on the road between San Antonio and Castroville, Schulter recruited someone to join him, and they headed out in search of the pair. He found them in D'Hanis, didn't believe the man's story that the boy belonged to him and, by threat of force, took them to the Medina County sheriff.

Soon thereafter, the mixed-race "boy" gave birth to "a fine male child." Meanwhile, the newspaper continued, the older male prisoner escaped, "carrying with him the animal he himself rode, a sorrel mare, and a black horse which had been ridden by the mulatto, together with the baggage which was strapped on the horse of the latter."

The new mother and child were returned to San Antonio, the newspaper said, "and are in charge of one of our citizens; she is described (now that she has got rid of her male habiliments) as being a remarkably good-looking mulatto girl of about nineteen years of age." The young woman told authorities that she and the man had left Missouri together the previous November, bound for Mexico, where slavery was illegal. With "the promised land almost in view," the article went on, "after all his toils and all his dangers, the old sinner must have felt it extremely annoying to have his dream of fancied security so rudely dispelled." Should the man be captured, the newspaper writer concluded, "it will go hard with him."

While a private citizen had ended the enslaved young woman's bid for freedom, beginning in 1853, Bexar County had a duly authorized slave patrol that was always on the lookout for runaways. The patrol was actually a contingent of eighteen district units covering all of the county, which, in the 1850s, was much larger in area than it is today. Interestingly, despite the predominant racial prejudices of the time, two of the eighteen patrol detachments were captained by Latinos. All of their men also were Latinos.

Slave patrols, used in the South as early as 1704, had been authorized by the Texas legislature on May 9, 1846, in "An Act to Provide for the Appointment of Patrols and to Prescribe Their Duties and Powers." Those powers were considerable. For instance, the patrols could come on to private property and conduct searches without a warrant. Further, the patrols could arrest runaway enslaved people and punish them with up to twenty-five lashes. White people who were believed to have assisted an enslaved person in escaping or were suspected of inciting enslaved people to revolt (a perennial southern fear prior to the Civil War) could also be summarily punished by the patrols.

Each patrol—the enslaved referred to them as "patterroles"—consisted of a captain and between three and five men, half of whom were to be owners or their agents. Service was compulsory, but each member was entitled under the law to their share of any reward posted by owners for the capture of a runaway.

A prayer credited to an old enslaved person in Clay County, Missouri, was as pertinent in Texas as it was in the Show Me State: "Oh, Lord, we thank thee for the New Jerusalem, with its pearly gates and its golden streets, but above all, we thank thee for that high wall around the great big city, so high that a patterroler can't get over it."

9
BIG HENRY

William Robertson Henry never knew his famous grandfather Patrick Henry, the Virginia rabble-rouser who, in 1775, famously declared, "I know not what course others may take; but as for me, give me liberty or give me death!" Even so, the younger Henry seems to have inherited his illustrious forebear's firebrand nature. And that would cost him the very thing his Patriot grandfather had been willing to gamble on—his life.

Born in 1822, Henry enlisted in the Second Regiment of Dragoons (forerunner of the Second Cavalry) in 1845 as tensions between the United States and Mexico grew following Texas's admission to the Union. When General Zachary Taylor was ordered to move troops into the new state, most of his army came to Texas by sea from New Orleans. The Second Dragoons, however, marched from Fort Jesup, Louisiana, to Corpus Christi on the mid-Texas coast. They made the five-hundred-mile trip in just over a month, reporting to Taylor in July 1845.

Following the war, during which Henry rose to the rank of sergeant, he decided to stay in Texas and settled in San Antonio. There, in the late fall of 1850, he married Consolacion Urrutia, and by the following year, Henry owned and operated a livery stable. A big man—in fact, "Big" was his nickname—in 1854, Henry was elected as a city marshal. Stout as he was, in a figurative sense, Big Henry's head was disproportionately larger than his body. Physician, newspaper editor and noted Texas Ranger John S. "Rip" Ford, who seldom lacked an opinion on anything, characterized Henry as a brave man with a large ego and little regard for authority.

This is how San Antonio looked in the 1850s, when William "Big" Henry walked the streets as the city marshal. *Author's collection.*

As the Alamo City's top cop, Henry occasionally arrested one of Texas's most notorious antebellum outlaws, Robert "Bob" Augustine. He was said to have killed a dozen men. While that's likely exaggerated, what is known is that while a sober Augustine could be charming, when drunk, he was as mean as a stepped-on rattlesnake. But in frontier Texas, the line between law enforcer and law breaker was easy to cross. Though Henry apparently had no qualms with putting Augustine in jail when he got too rowdy, the marshal either began to like Augustine or at least admired his known skills with a gun.

In March 1855, Henry resigned as marshal and was commissioned as a Ranger captain. But scouting for hostile Native Americans did not offer the opportunities that participating in a revolution south of the Rio Grande might bring. If Henry could assist the governor of the Mexican state of Chihuahua in his rebellious aspirations, he may have reasoned that he might end up with a high military rank or an even greater position of power. The Ranger captain offered the governor his assistance, only to be told, in effect, thanks but no thanks. Though he was still on the muster roll as a Ranger captain, Henry soon tried to team up with another ambitious state leader in Mexico. Again, his offer was rejected.

Not long after, he led some forty fellow filibusterers—Rangers or ex-Rangers—across the border intending to start his own revolution. However, one researcher believes Henry was more interested in capturing escaped enslaved people in Mexico and returning them to Texas for the reward money than in fomenting revolution. Whatever his true motivation, Henry and his command were taken into custody by Mexican troops and escorted back to the river.

In September 1855, Henry got another chance to splash across the Rio Grande, this time as second-in-command of a punitive force under Ranger captain James Callahan. When Henry recruited men for the company he would lead, twenty-two-year-old Bob Augustine enlisted. The Texans rode into Mexico intent on fighting Native Americans, though an independent historian who wrote a well-researched book on Callahan believes the so-called Callahan expedition was more about private gain than an effort to curtail Native American raids from across the border. Instead of clashing with Native Americans, they ended up fighting with Mexican troops. The main thing Callahan and Henry succeeded in doing was getting back to Texas alive.

After returning to San Antonio, Henry was elected sheriff of Bexar County and took office on August 4, 1856. Former Ranger Augustine, however, returned to his old ways and soon found himself in the county jail. This time, Augustine had committed a crime that netted him a five-year prison sentence. But before he could be transferred to the state penitentiary in Huntsville, he escaped the hoosegow in the fall of 1856. Sheriff Henry was indicted by a Bexar County grand jury for "allowing a prisoner to escape," but the charge was later dismissed, and Henry went on to complete his two-year term.

Recaptured in New Orleans in early 1858, Augustine was taken straight to prison. Henry, meanwhile, left for Nicaragua with filibuster William A. Walker. Surviving that debacle, he returned to Texas and, in 1859, once again enlisted as a Ranger. This time, he joined fellow San Antonian William G. Tobin, serving on the border in Tobin's company until 1860.

When the Civil War broke out in 1861, chaos and near anarchy reigned in San Antonio as federal troops left the state and most Texas men of fighting age enlisted in the Confederate army. Meanwhile, having served his time, Bob Augustine was back in town and again causing trouble. On September 7, 1861, San Antonio residents decided they'd had enough of the outlaw. After he appeared in court on a disorderly conduct charge, as soon as he emerged from the courthouse, Augustine was seized and hanged.

Since Henry may have been complicit in helping Augustine escape jail five years earlier, whether he witnessed or participated in the lynching is not known. What is known is that Henry wanted to get back in the Rangers, which Texas's Confederate government needed to patrol the frontier to discourage Native American incursions. Coveting another captaincy, Big Henry's chance came early in 1862, when a Ranger company that had been assigned to Fort Davis in far West Texas was ordered to return to San Antonio.

Henry apparently began politicking to replace the current captain, well-to-do Bandera County rancher William C. Adams. Henry was saying things about Adams, and evidently, Adams didn't spare the trash talk concerning Henry. Whether it was over perceived slander or done with the intention to get Adams out of the picture so he could take over the company, on March 15, Henry decided to challenge Adams to a duel.

Though he was known as an effective peace officer, the forty-year-old Henry seems to have fallen into dissipation. He was known to be a heavy drinker, and earlier that day, Henry had pleaded guilty to two counts of gambling and was assessed a twenty-five-dollar fine. Strangely, possibly because he had been in court earlier that day, Henry was not armed. Seeing an acquaintance named Hiram Mitchell in a billiard parlor, Henry grabbed the man's revolver and said, "I want it about fifteen minutes." Hefting the handgun, he asked Mitchell if it was "well-loaded," and Mitchell said that there were two balls in one chamber. When Henry stuck the gun inside his waistband and started for the door of the saloon, Mitchell followed him outside.

Mitchell saw Adams walking down the street toward Henry. The two men spoke, and then Adams shook hands with Henry. Despite the friendly gesture, Henry put his hand on the handle of his borrowed revolver and said to Adams, "I can whip you on the plaza." Adams said that he would be glad to meet him there but that he was not a fighting man. At that, Henry told Adams he was a fighting man "and as brave as Julius Caesar." Clearly wishing to avoid any conflict, Adams began walking away.

As another witness related, "Henry told Adams then that he was a coward and a liar and that if he met him on the street again, he would shoot two balls through his head."

"What did you say?" Adams asked. Henry again said he would "give him some six-shooter balls."

"I will fight you now," Adams replied.

At that, Mitchell grabbed Henry to hold him back, but Henry shoved him away and told him not to "molest" him. Henry then drew his pistol, and Mitchell ducked for cover. Henry fired first, followed an instant later by Adams, who shot twice. Henry, who had missed Adams, fell to the ground and soon died. Adams then asked where the sheriff's office was, saying he wanted to turn himself in.

In early April, a six-man coroner's jury determined after hearing testimony from four witnesses that "W.R. Henry came to his death by two balls fired at him by one Captain W.B. Adams taking effect in his breast and head, which was done in self-defense."

Henry may have been as brave as Caesar but must not have remembered that March 15, the day he chose to demonstrate his fearlessness, just happened to be the Ides of March, the date of the Roman emperor's assassination.

10

MURDERED FOR A WAGONLOAD OF BUFFALO MEAT

On the morning of Tuesday, February 27, 1878, Herman Potchuskey and Herman Stappenbeck headed to the San Antonio River to see if the fish were biting. Not long after they arrived, somewhere between 8:00 and 9:00 a.m., Potchuskey saw something floating in the water. Thinking it a log, but not entirely sure, he tossed in a hefty rock. That created enough of a splash to reveal that the object was the body of a man floating face-down.

Potchuskey ran to notify authorities. Soon, City Marshal John Dobbin, Constable Fred Bader and other officers arrived. "The [body] seemed to be those of an old man about 120 pounds," Bader later testified. "The head had been crushed. It had not been done by a gunshot wound but done with a blunt or heavy instrument." Clearly, as a newspaper later reported, the man found in the river "had been foully done with."

Looking to be about fifty years old, the man wore an old blue army coat with brass buttons and brown pants. He had nothing in his pockets offering any clues to his identity, and no one in the large crowd that had gathered recognized him as a local resident. Officers and onlookers searched up and down the river for any possible evidence but found nothing that would seem to be connected to the crime. Meanwhile, officers removed the body from the water. They loaded it into a wagon, and Constable Bader took it to the poorhouse, which had a cemetery for paupers. The body was placed in a plain coffin and buried.

The next day, a man named William Patterson approached Marshal Dobbin and said a friend of his, a buffalo hunter named Peter Maddox, was missing. Patterson said he'd heard that a body had been found in the river and feared it might be that of Maddox. The concerned friend told the marshal that he'd last seen Maddox on Sunday, when Maddox and another man he did not know arrived in San Antonio from a buffalo hunt along the Concho River, about 250 miles to the northwest. Both men sat on an ox-drawn wagon piled high with buffalo hides and dried meat. At one point, Maddox pulled Patterson aside and quietly asked him to stay with him, saying he believed the other, younger man intended to rob and kill him. Patterson thought his friend was "probably more timid than there was any real occasion for and did not remain with them."

On Monday, Patterson continued, he had gone looking for his friend at the market plaza but could not find him. He spoke with the man he'd seen with Maddox, whom he had found at the main plaza with buffalo meat for sale at eight cents a pound. When Patterson asked the man where he could find his friend, he made a show of looking around and said he was around there somewhere but didn't know where. Patterson told the man to tell Maddox he was looking for him and left.

Thinking Maddox may have been correct in his concern that his partner meant him harm, the marshal went to the plaza and arrested the man on suspicion of murder. His name was Jacob E. "Jake" Hainline. Searching the wagon, he found an axe with traces of what appeared to be blood on it and some quilts that also looked bloodstained.

After consulting with Justice of the Peace Cotton, the marshal got an order to exhume the body that had been found in the river so Patterson could make a positive identification. While that was routine enough, the lawman did something a bit more unorthodox—he took the suspect to view the body as well.

At the poorhouse, the day-old grave was uncovered, and the coffin opened. There was no question, Patterson said in so many words, that the body was that of his friend. Though the sight of the corpse had shaken Patterson, Hainline showed no reaction. He didn't know the man, he said. When reminded that Patterson had seen him with Maddox, Hainline said, "Well, yes. On second thought, the body might be Maddox's," but he had no idea how the man had met his death.

Believing Hainline knew exactly what had happened to Maddox, the marshal took the suspect to jail while the victim was reburied. The next day, however, the body was dug up a second time so three doctors could

Two buffalo hunters headed for San Antonio in 1878 to sell dried meat in Main Plaza, but one only one of them made it all the way to town. *Author's collection.*

examine it. When comparing the suspected murder weapon with the wounds to Maddox's skull, the physicians and officers agreed that they matched perfectly. Maddox, they believed, had been lying face-down, likely asleep, when someone used the heavy backside of an axe blade to crush his skull. The victim was then reburied for the third and final time.

"The evidence [against Hainline] is overwhelming," a correspondent for the *Galveston Daily News* wrote from the Alamo City. After hearing that evidence, a jury agreed with the newspaper's assessment. The panel found Hainline guilty and further concluded he should hang for his crime. His attorneys appealed the conviction, but as one newspaper later reported, "the verdict was not disturbed."

Shortly before their client's execution date, Hainline's attorneys released a lengthy statement from the defendant that maintained it was really Patterson who killed Maddox, not him. No one took that seriously, though it made for a sensational newspaper article.

At 11:05 a.m. on August 6, 1879, Hainline—accompanied by two priests—was led from his cell to the well-used Bexar County gallows elsewhere in the jail. Described by reporters as "cool and collected," Hainline showed no emotion as a deputy adjusted the noose around his neck. When asked if he had any last words, he said he had nothing to say other than that he did not begrudge the officers who were about to hang him, that they had taken good care of him while he was in jail. A deputy then placed a black mask over his face and stepped back. When the trapdoor sprang, the seven-foot drop broke his neck, but thirteen minutes passed before doctors said his heart stopped beating. "The execution was admirably managed in all particulars," the *Galveston Daily News* observed at the end of its report.

11

A NO-ACCOUNT COUNT OR NAIVE NOBLEMAN?

For a landlocked city, San Antonio has always had a cosmopolitan air. By the 1860s, the three principal population groups—about evenly divided—were Anglos, Mexicans and first- or second-generation German immigrants. The Alamo City also had a fair number of French-speaking residents, given its proximity to Castroville, a town in Medina County that was settled in the 1840s by colonists from the French province of Alsace.

The French presence in the area may have been what attracted a handsome young Frenchman to San Antonio in late 1879 or early 1880. Very much the gentleman, the visitor's name was Count Charles Dodun de Keroman. Dashing, well-educated and titled, de Keroman made friends easily with men and attractive young ladies. Whether born of naivety, a sense of entitlement or genuine criminal intent, he was arrested for burglary in Kerr County, sixty-five miles northwest of San Antonio. After quickly making bond, the count returned to San Antonio, where he became acquainted with some of the city's most prosperous and proper residents. At some point, he traveled to France for a time, but he returned to San Antonio.

When he got off the train at the Southern Pacific depot, he was met by French businessman Jean LaCoste and Dr. George Cupples. The doctor was a Scotsman, but had been in Texas since 1844, when it was still an independent republic. As Keroman later recalled, Dr. Cupples "proposed that I should become a guest at his house, which invitation I accepted."

Downtown San Antonio during the brief "reign" of a French count with an eye for the ladies. *Portal of Texas History*.

Though he was in his sixties, the doctor had married a younger woman following the death of his first wife. The new Mrs. Cupples (née Laura Lagrave Sheahan) had an attractive daughter, Katie. Not surprisingly, it did not take long for Katie and the count to become enamored with each other. When the count made another trip to his native country, he returned with an engagement ring for Katie. But sticking to proper decorum, the count first asked Dr. Cupples for his daughter's hand in marriage, and the doctor readily assented.

Seven months later, the count and the doctor got into an argument over international politics. Neither debater budging in his position; as the count put it, "I took my hat and remarked, 'I will leave your house, doctor, as you have insulted my country." If the count hoped for an apology from his erstwhile host, it was not forthcoming. Not only that, but Cupples told him not to come back.

Not long afterward, the count left by train for New Orleans and eventually France. "Our popular friend, Count de Keroman, left on February 8 for Paris," the *San Antonio Light* reported. "The people of San Antonio have become very much interested in and attached to Count Keroman," the newspaper continued, "and all wish him a successful arrangement of his business affairs in France and a speedy return to our country, which he intends making his home hereafter." The same snippet also noted that the count, during his stay in San Antonio, "has deservedly made many friends, and the people of our community wish him to permanently locate here."

When the count's business in France was completed, he returned to San Antonio in late April "in fine health and spirits." What the count did for a living was never mentioned by the local newspapers, but his family clearly had money.

In July 1881, Keroman defied Dr. Cupples's enjoinder that he never show up again at his residence. Reading between the lines in the newspaper coverage that followed, Keroman had come to reclaim the jewelry he'd given to his former fiancée. While there, what the newspapers would later call "a difficulty" occurred between Keroman and the doctor.

Five months later, the count was arrested on January 31, 1882, charged with the aggravated assault of Mrs. Cupples and her daughter. In addition, he was charged with assault with intent to murder Dr. Cupples and with the verbal assault of the Cupples family's coachman, G.F. Dale. Bond was set at $300 for each count, and the district attorney's office began preparing to present the evidence to the Bexar County Grand Jury.

"The difficulty between Dr. Cupples and Count de Keroman is generally talked over," the *Light* noted on February 1, "and there is a great deal of foolish talk about it. For the sake of all parties, we hope the matter may be dropped, as a public examination will bring to light a great deal more for people to talk about, and any further complication of the row will force the newspapers to give the facts as they get them."

The filing of charges against the count made national news. "It is said that a great scandal will be developed when the matter comes before the court," a St. Louis newspaper reported.

The evening *San Antonio Times* interviewed Dr. Cupples and published his version of what happened. Unfortunately for posterity, that newspaper soon folded, and its back issues were apparently not preserved. But the *Times*'s afternoon rival, the *Light*, weighed in with a long interview of the count, who told his story in a lengthy page-one article that appeared on February 4.

In the interview, the count maintained that the doctor's wife had not agreed with her husband on barring the count from their home. When the doctor was away, the count said Mrs. Cupples allowed him to call on her daughter. But when the count found out that Katie's mother had also allowed another gentlemen caller to take her daughter in his buggy to San Pedro Springs, he was not pleased. "I became excited," he told the *Light*'s reporter, "knowing that Mrs. Cupples sought to arouse my jealousy. I may not have been polite in my expressions to Mrs. Cupples, but positively deny having made the slightest assault upon her." When Katie tried to intervene, as the count put it, "I put her aside with no view of inflicting the slightest personal injury." At that point, Katie "asked that all that had transpired should be forgotten and that I should ask Mrs. Cupples's pardon, which I did." Mrs. Cupples said she was willing to overlook the count's treatment of her, but not what he had said to her daughter (which was not reported).

The incident apparently ended the count's romance with Katie, but that turned out to be only the first act. In October 1881, the pair began seeing each other again. The count told the newspaper that it was "with the consent and approval of the mother." Dr. Cupples, however, did not approve. He may not have even known about it until he came home one day in July 1881. That led to a ruckus, which, depending on the teller, involved either the count threatening to kill the carriage man, the doctor threatening to kill the count or the count threatening to kill the doctor.

Though Dr. Cupples had pressed charges against the count, he apparently concluded it was in his family's best interest to not pursue the matter. When a justice of the peace convened an examining trial on February 8, attorneys representing both sides were present, but none of the pertinent witnesses were there. The judge reset the case for February 18, but on the motion of the state, the charges against the count were dismissed prior to the hearing.

"The dismissal of the charges looks like a cruel sell upon the public and a very serious joke upon the count, who has been published far and wide as a woman beater and a bad man," the *Light* observed on February 16. "The collapse of this matter leaves some awkward situations."

Why did everyone involved—the Cupples family, the district attorney's office and local newspapers—think it best that the matter be dropped? In his long interview with the *Light*, the count made mention of a cache of letters he and Katie had exchanged. Perhaps some of the sentiments expressed in the correspondence were too sensitive for Victorian sensibilities. Or maybe there was even more to it. The "great scandal" predicted by newspapers had been averted, surely much to the regret of many of their readers.

Whatever happened between the count and Katie, it didn't take the good-looking Frenchman long to find someone else who was interested in becoming a countess. His new love was Julia Barratte, whose father owned a restaurant in the Alamo City. They were married in the summer of 1882 in Orange on the Texas-Louisiana border and then left to honeymoon in New Orleans. A brief mention of the nuptials in the *Light* noted that the couple had been engaged for some time.

While he had wed a San Antonio belle, the count seemed to have had enough of the Alamo City. The couple settled in New Orleans, where Keroman worked at the consulate until he and his wife moved to Panama. That was, as the *Light* reported on June 19, 1883, to assume "the important position of superintendent in the building of the Panama Canal."

An accomplished competitive fencer, the count's skill with a rapier offered no protection from disease. On November 26, 1883, his father-in-law in San Antonio received a cable from his daughter: the count had died that morning of yellow fever. The next day, the *San Antonio Light* devoted only seven lines to the news. "The count is well known in this city for several reasons," the newspaper noted discretely, "one being his marriage with Miss Barratte, daughter of one of our oldest citizens." "Deceased," the *San Antonio Express* opined in a brief death notice a few days later, "was a wild and adventurous character…[who had] made some narrow escapes from the clutches of the law." Whether Keroman was just a no-account count or a young nobleman who could have gone on to greater things remains an open question.

12

THE REDEMPTION OF WILLIAM CHRYSLER

With its scores of wide-open saloons, the booming 1880s San Antonio had no shortage of falling-down drunks. But William Chrysler had the dubious distinction of being the town drunk, an alcoholic whom bar owners, officers of the law, the city recorder's court, journalists and the general public couldn't help but like.

Several characteristics separated Chrysler—a man in his sixties with gray hair and a lined face—from other barflies. For one, he came from a good Texas family. Beyond that, he was a skilled mechanic (as carpenters back then often were referred to) particularly known for his furniture making. Funny, intelligent and personable, Chrysler was so well known in the Alamo City that newspaper reporters who wrote of his antics didn't feel it necessary to go into detail about his background, other than to occasionally note that he owned a furniture store at the corner of Market Street and Main Plaza, or that at some point he had been a judge in Calhoun County. But as for formal legal training, the only bar he ever approached was his favorite watering hole, and if he'd really ever been a judge, he was seldom sober as one.

San Antonio's daily newspapers, keenly though collegially competitive, chronicled every aspect of life—and death—in the city. Reporters daily checked hotel registers and funeral parlors, hung out at the depots to see who was arriving or departing and checked court dockets and other public records, from marriage licenses and divorce petitions to real estate transactions. Every day, a reporter for the *Express* and its rival the *Light* were present in the recorder's court—the equivalent of today's municipal courts—to cover the proceedings.

Years later, longtime *Express* reporter Fred Mosebach, who cut his reportorial teeth covering the recorder's court, put the misdemeanor court into perspective: "The police court [also known as the recorder's court] has always been a sort of clearing house for mischief, such for instance as when somebody falls off the water wagon. For drollery and downright comedy, there are scenes in police court that cannot be matched on the stage or screen."

When Chrysler's name first started showing up in the newspapers, the coverage was perfunctory, merely noting his name, what he had been arrested for (generally for being "drunk and disorderly") and how much his fine was. However, there were occasional hints that Chrysler stood out from most miscreants. "Our recorder has had before him several times of late two men once prominent in the affairs of the country, but who have, through the excessive use of strong drink, descended to that sphere of depravity where all respect is lost and all decency forgotten," the *Express* noted on March 20, 1881. One of those men was Chrysler, and the other was a friend of his, also originally from Calhoun County.

Less than a year later, on May 1, 1882, the *Light* noted that a hefty fine imposed on Chrysler had been "remitted on account of good behavior."

William Chrysler achieved notoriety as the town drunk before he decided to run for city court judge. He spent a lot of time in what locals called the "Bat Cave," the two-story jail in the center of this image. *Author's collection.*

That summer, under a headline reading "Les Misérables" the *Light* reported that Chrysler, "a gentlemen who has seen better days," had been fined fifteen dollars for a drunken spat.

When the August 29, 1883 edition of the *Light* rolled off the press, it carried a page-one story headlined, "Judge Chrysler/How the Audiences in the Recorder's Court Were Amused This Morning." The article explained that the recorder, having been out late celebrating recent local election results, had not shown up for docket call that morning. "Prisoners were waiting with anxious faces," the newspaper said, "police and lawyers were getting impatient, and the members of the press were holding a solemn conclave as to what should be done." They waited a bit longer, but still no one arrived to preside over the court.

"Suddenly," the newspaper continued, "an officer with beaming countenance" rose to propose the ad hoc appointment of a special judge. "There is one here worthy to take the seat of the high and mighty Mogul," the officer said. "Yes, one right here…William Chrysler."

Officers and reporters "hurried him to the chair," despite Chrysler's modest protestations that he was not qualified for such an important position. Having been duly if not legally appointed to the bench, Chrysler brought up the first case, "City of San Antonio vs. William Chrysler, charged with inebriation." The judge began:

> *As I know the gentleman, his habits, eccentricities, weaknesses and virtues, it would be a work of supererogation to enter upon a trial, and since he had no criminal intent, an indispensable element of guilt, and although his example is neither to be commended nor followed, I shall give him a chance to reform, and upon his promise to leave town, I shall dismiss the case. Mr. Chrysler, if you are here tomorrow, I will both try you and fine you.*

"Judge" Chrysler then took judicial notice of the officer who had arrested him. "Let us try the police officer Bishop for arresting one William Chrysler," the judge said. At that, he promptly found the officer guilty and assessed his fine at twenty-five dollars. But then, demonstrating his judicious nature, Chrysler told the defendant that the court would remit the fine "on the promise that you stand drinks." According to the *Light*'s account of the proceedings, the officer accepted the judgment of the court, and as soon as the rest of the docket had been handled, the court, police, former defendants and the press left the Bat Cave for the White Elephant Saloon.

While it is hard to believe that being appointed to the bench by a police officer had any legal standing, the newspapers nevertheless reported it as a fact. Likely, the mayor and the duly elected recorder enjoyed the stunt.

As for Judge Chrysler, contrary to his own order, he did not quit drinking to excess or anything else. Back in the spring of 1884, again charged with drunkenness, the case was passed over by the recorder "on the fervid promises of the accused never to drink again." Chrysler never drank again until May 13, when he was arrested for "cursing and swearing." As the *Light* explained, "Mr. Chrysler received a day or two since some remuneration for being cook to the convict camp and spent some of it in getting drunk. A further draft of five dollars on his newly acquired resources was made by the recorder." Three days later, Chrysler was back in jail again, "charged with his usual offense." Again fined five dollars, he surrendered half that amount before being remanded to jail to lay out the rest of the fine. He was arrested again for drunkenness on May 18 and again on May 25.

One of the incidents that netted him yet another trip to the Bat Cave was his "assault" of a cigar store Indian. Evidently in good shape for a man in his age, Chrysler knocked the wooden carving off its base into the muddy street and wrestled with it until one of San Antonio's finest arrived to rescue the defenseless brave.

Back in court on July 7, Chrysler pleaded that his drunkenness was only due to observing the Fourth of July. If the recorder had been moved by the familiar defendant's patriotism, he still fined him five dollars.

Chrysler was back in the news only two weeks later. Once again, he had been arrested for his usual offense and escorted in handcuffs to the Bat Cave. "The rascal," the *Light* said, "after his arrival there, scaled the wall and effected an escape. A *Light* reporter saw the old man this morning on a San Pedro [streetcar], with a placid smile on his face. W.C. informed the reporter he was going west."

"W.C." must not have gone too far west, because on August 22, 1884, he was arrested by Alamo City officers for vagrancy. When Chrysler appeared in court the next day, the recorder dismissed the complaint and told "the old gentleman" to go to work.

Busted again for "being drunk upon the streets," on May 9, 1885, Chrysler surprised the court by pleading not guilty and asking for a jury trial. Based on his previous judicial experience, not to mention his accumulated courtroom acumen, Chrysler announced that he would serve as his own lawyer. The recorder ordered the bailiff to round up a jury, and the city attorney put on two witnesses who testified concerning Chrysler's latest spree. "The case looked quite gloomy for Chrysler until he arose to make a speech, which he did, addressing the jury in plain, straight-forward style that won their sympathy and caused them to bring in a verdict of not guilty."

Chrysler, who the *Light* described as "the poor old man who is a slave to liquor," was arrested several more times in 1885, but beginning that summer, he spent most of his time in Gonzales doing carpentry work. When he returned to San Antonio in February 1886, an *Express* reporter noted he was "sober as a judge, and...says he has not tussled with John Barleycorn for several months."

After that, Chrysler's name did not appear in print until January 20, 1887, when the *Light* noted that the reformed alcoholic had announced that he would be seeking election as the next city recorder. The newspaper said he had received pledges of support "from a great number of good citizens."

One February 12, the *Express* published a lengthy editorial endorsement of Chrysler for recorder. Calling him "a man of more than ordinary intellectual attainments, of patriotic impulses, and liberal and public spirited in character," the editorial went on to note that "while recognized as one of the leading and most useful citizens of western Texas," he had been "beset by misfortunes and went down." But the editorial continued, Chrysler had finally put the proverbial plug in the jug. "I have taken my last drink," one reporter later remembered Chrysler declaring, "and I hope to see the day when whisky will be wiped out of existence." Despite the endorsement of both dailies, Chrysler lost the election. Even so, his newfound sobriety had made him a winner no matter the ballot count.

"Chrysler," *Express* reporter Mosebach recalled, "like all inebriates when they banish booze, became a teetotaler and took up the cause of Prohibition with a vengeance. He delivered lectures on the evils of drink and denounced liquor as the most terrible curse of man."

The reformation of William Chrysler did not last. On May 2, 1889, under the newspaper's standing "Recorder's Court" headline, with no sidebar comments, the *Light* merely noted: "William Chrysler, drunk and disorderly, five dollars." While that seems to have been the last time Chrysler ever sat at what the newspaper's referred to as "the mourner's bench" at the recorder's court, the "judge's" dissipation apparently continued. On December 2, 1889, the *Light* noted tersely: "William Chrysler, seventy years old, died this morning after an illness of several weeks."

13
THE MISSING SIX-SHOOTER

Whatever became of Ben Thompson's six-shooter?

Thompson, a British-born former Texas Ranger and soldier of fortune with a penchant for booze and gambling, made quite a reputation as city marshal of Austin in the early 1880s. His life ended violently in San Antonio on the night of March 11, 1884, when someone gunned him down along with former outlaw-turned-lawman King Fisher of Uvalde. The already legendary shootist crumpled to the floor with his six-shooter smoking, but the weapon he clutched in his hand when he died cannot be accounted for today.

Though neither Thompson nor Fisher could claim to be a church deacon, they had not been looking for trouble that evening. They were just two gentlemen out on the town in the Alamo City, taking in a variety show after dinner along with numerous drinks. But Thompson had a well-known temper, particularly when in his cups. A verbal sparring match led to Thompson slapping Joe Foster, the former business partner of the late Jack Harris, the founder of the establishment where they stood, Jack Harris's Vaudeville Theatre and Saloon. Moments later, lead started flying.

No matter the exact circumstances of what happened that evening, it didn't take Sherlock Holmes to deduce that it had something to do with the fact that Thompson had killed Harris back on July 11, 1882. Charged with the murder, he had been acquitted.

In the shooting of Thompson and Fisher, the coroner's verdict concluded they died "from the effects of pistol shot wounds from pistols held and fired

Ben Thompson had served as the Austin city marshal, but his life ended violently in San Antonio in the early spring of 1884. *Author's collection.*

from the hands of J.C. Foster [who later died of the wound he received in the fight] and Jacobo S. Coy…and that the said killing was justifiable and done in self-defense in the immediate danger of life."

Former newspaperman and San Antonio historian Sam Wolford told Thompson's story in a speech to a group of military historians at Fort Sam Houston on November 18, 1953. The Witte Museum, where Woolford served as an honorary curator of history, later published his remarks in a seventeen-page pamphlet with a small press run. "There are countless gun collectors in the United States, and you know how much they would pay to own the six-shooter they took off Ben Thompson's body that night," he told his audience.

Black powder smoke still hanging in the air, just about every law enforcement officer in San Antonio rushed to the scene of the shooting that night. The ranking officers included San Antonio marshal Phil Shardein and Bexar County sheriff's captain T.P. McCall (McCall was later elected Bexar County sheriff, serving from January 1, 1889, to December 31, 1892). Also on hand was deputy William Krempkau, a former trail driver.

One of the participants, special police officer Coy, later said in a sworn affidavit that he turned Thompson's pistol over to Shardein that night. "I examined it without revolving the cylinder and discovered that five shots had been fired," Shardein said in his statement. "The cylinder has been moved since it was in my possession. When I had it, the loaded cartridge was next to the barrel, and cocking it would have thrown the cartridge under the hammer." In other words, for safety reasons, the marshal either moved the cylinder or took out the shell. (Removing the shell would have been their best bet.) At some point, Shardein turned Thompson's pistol over to future sheriff McCall.

Historians are not even 100 percent sure what caliber revolver Thompson was packing that night. Unfortunately, no one in authority seems to have recorded the weapon's serial number, long since standard police procedure in a criminal investigation. One writer, not offering a source, said the pistol in question was a pearl-handled, nickel-plated .45-caliber pistol.

The hard-drinking Thompson and his friend King Fisher were shot to death in Jack Harris's Variety Theater. *Author's collection.*

While that may have been the case, two years earlier, when Thompson killed Harris, the record shows he used a pistol chambered for .44-caliber rounds, a popular Old West cartridge that could be used in a handgun or Winchester rifle. "He bought ten cents' worth, that is five cartridges," San Antonio gun store owner Charles F.A. Hummel testified after the Harris killing. "They were central [center] fire forty-four-caliber."

Former deputy Krempkau could have answered the question as to the caliber and style of the piece Thompson carried on his last night of life. Only a young man at the time of the Thompson-Fisher killing, Krempkau later ran San Antonio's Barrel House Saloon. "Uncle Billy," as he came to be called, lived well into the twentieth century. By the 1940s, he could claim to be the last principal in the case who was still kicking.

"Billy, whatever happened to Ben Thompson's gun," Wolford asked one day, hoping to land it for display in the Witte. "Oh, after Captain McCall gave me the gun, it lay around the house for a few years, and I finally sold it to a Mexican for ten dollars," the former deputy said.

For the next decade, Wolford pestered Krempkau, trying to get him to remember the name of the man. To Wolford's lasting dismay, Krempkau never managed to retrieve the name from his memory. The former deputy died on October 11, 1953, and was buried in San Antonio's old City Cemetery.

Kurt House, a former curator of San Antonio's famed Buckhorn Saloon Museum, has done considerable research on Thompson. But other than having a faint recollection that the late Tom Keilman may have auctioned a pistol supposedly once owned by Thompson, he does not know if that was Thompson's death gun or its location today.

14

LAW AND ORDER AT THE ALAMO

Since its construction began in 1744, the Alamo has been a mission chapel, a hospital, a makeshift fortification, a U.S. military supply depot, a storage building and, finally, a historical landmark. What hardly anyone knows is that during San Antonio's wildest and wooliest days, the shrine of Texas liberty accommodated a police station.

The old Spanish chapel had been remodeled by the U.S. Army in 1848 (which is when the Alamo's façade got its iconic hump) and used by the military until the establishment of Fort Sam Houston in 1876. At some point in the late 1870s, likely as San Antonio began to boom after getting its first rail connection in 1877, the city marshal (then tantamount to police chief) established a police substation at the Alamo so officers could better maintain law and order on Alamo Plaza and all of the city on the east side of the river.

The facility referred to at the time as Alamo Station or the Alamo Police Station was not located inside the old Spanish church but occupied a one-story, two-room frame structure that stood in the half rectangle formed by the three sides of the chapel's southern wall. Documentation is scanty to nonexistent, but it appears that the structure had been built for some other purpose and later leased to the city. Whatever its origin, there is no doubt that it once served San Antonio's finest. A Sanborn insurance map produced in 1885 shows a structure unambiguously labeled "Police Station" nestled between the old baptistry (in the chapel's southwest corner) and the transept.

The Alamo Police Station was essentially a precinct house with a small office and adjoining holding room where prisoners could be confined until they were transferred by wagon to the "Bat Cave," the 1852 vintage city-county law enforcement building and jail on Military Plaza.

Nineteenth-century newspapers primarily concerned themselves with crime news and didn't pay as much attention to law enforcement methodologies or infrastructure. But contemporary newspaper articles reflect that the department kept at least two mounted officers at the substation, a day shift and a night shift officer. The substation had a telephone so officers could communicate with headquarters and take calls from the public.

In 1885, City Marshal Phil Shardein commanded a thirty-two-person force. The department was not heavy on administration. Shardein had a deputy marshal as second-in-command and a second assistant city marshal. Except for a jailer and two court officers, everyone else had a badge. Five years later, the city council voted in February 1890 to add eight officers to the force. That gave the department "the active strength of...about fifty, the largest constabulary of any city in Texas." Those officers were making seventy-five dollars a month.

On a rotating basis, at least two mounted police officers were assigned to the Alamo station per twelve-hour shift. They may not have relished the assignment, given the station's small size and state of disrepair. However, things improved in early 1894. "The Alamo police station has received several needed improvements," the *Light* noted on January 25. "A washstand has been placed in the small room, and a clothes rack has been made. Several rat holes have been stopped up with tin. A large stove has been put up, and the officers on duty...are now comfortably situated."

Officers assigned to the station remained busy. In May 1894, for example, they made forty-three arrests for violations ranging from vagrancy and disorderly conduct to failure to pay city occupation taxes. Total arrests citywide for the month were 311.

When the Alamo station began operations, only four decades had passed since the historic battle that occurred there. While it would be years before it transitioned from an old building to a shrine, the officers who worked out of the substation were well aware that a lot of people died there. And where there have been nonpeaceful deaths, ghost stories soon arise.

Making his rounds on the morning of January 31, a reporter for the *Light* learned of strange goings-on at the station. Somewhere between 11:00 p.m. and midnight the day before, an Officer Keron was alone in the substation when he began hearing strange noises. Reading a newspaper while two of his fellow officers were out on a call, "he heard the voice of a woman in the adjoining room, and making an investigation, found nothing." A short

For more than a decade, a small nineteenth-century addition to the Alamo accommodated a police substation. *Author's collection.*

time later, the article continued, saying Keron "heard a woman crying and then heard the footsteps of a man overhead." At that, the newspaper went on, "he became frightened and left the building." When his colleagues returned, they searched the area but found no one. Later that night, both officers also heard sounds they couldn't explain. "The readers who have their doubts about the facts above stated are cordially invited to the Alamo station between the hours of 11 and 1 o'clock any night, and they will be convinced," the reporter concluded.

Captain Jacobo Coy, a longtime police officer whose captaincy was only honorary, was nevertheless the person in charge at the Alamo station on the evening of February 3, 1894, when Leon Mareschal, "an old and respected citizen," showed up with his fourteen-year-old daughter, Mary. Mareschal explained that he was not in need of any police services but thought he could be of service to the department. What they could do, Mareschal said, was communicate with ghosts.

"Captain Coy gave the parties two chairs and permitted them to use the little jail room adjoining the station office," the *Express* reported two days later. "Mr. Mareschal placed his daughter in a trance and told Captain Coy to speak to the spirits through the medium." Whether the officer really believed the young girl could "speak" with ghosts or if he was merely playing along on a slow night is unknowable today, but according to the newspaper, Coy asked the girl if she could see "the spirits."

"Yes," she replied, "they are men."

"Then get them to form a line, and ask them who they are," the captain said.

At that, Mary "nervously twitched her head from side to side" and told Coy they had fallen in line. "The forms say that they are the spirits of the defenders of the Alamo," she continued. Coy did not press further but asked, "What is the object of their visit and noise in the building at night?" Mary remained silent for a second or two before saying, "They say that there is buried in the walls of the building $50,000 in $20 gold pieces. They also say that they are anxious to have the money discovered and have been waiting for a chance to communicate with the people on Earth about it and have it discovered. They will relinquish all claim to the treasure in favor of the person who finds it." Then the officer asked the obvious question: "Where in the building?"

"It's in the wall near that room," Mary said, pointing toward the old baptistry. "It's in the wall at that—" Her trance had broken. By then, it was well past midnight, and Mareschal took his daughter home. "Those who believe in spiritualism lay considerable confidence in the result of Miss Mareschal's interview with the spirits," the *Express* observed, "and it is currently reported that the local psychical society will investigate the alleged phenomenon."

Following the publication of the story, rumor spread that the city's police officers were afraid to be inside the Alamo station at night. After all, six-shooters offered no protection from someone who was already dead. That prompted four soldiers, presumably on their own time, to show up at the station to offer their services as guards. "Their offer was declined with thanks," the article concluded.

Haunts weren't the only issue facing officers stationed at the Alamo. On August 3, 1894, the *Light* reported that an officer who worked at the station "has been laid up for several days from illness contracted by smelling the foul ditch that runs by the Alamo police station." In late May, the newspaper had reported that the "stench emenating from the open Alamo ditch near the Alamo police station is quite unbearable. A sanitary inspector will investigate."

The notion that the Alamo might be haunted gained further traction in the fall of 1895, when, on November 23, the city jail's prisoners who were being used to tear up the floor in a small room adjoining the station dug up part of a human skull in one corner of the room. "It is believed the skull is one of Texas's noble heroes who sacrificed his life in freeing the Lone

Star state from Mexico. When the prisoner saw the skull, he immediately quit digging at that place, for fear, as he said, he might strike the rest of the skeleton." Once the project had been completed, the room was used to shelter police horses during the winter.

For whatever reason, in the spring of 1896, the Alamo station was moved to East Houston Street across from the post office. What use was made of the vacated building after that is not known, but photographs of the Alamo from the early 1900s show that the wooden addition was no longer there.

15

COCKFIGHTING

Rumor is a thing than can quickly get out of hand.

Reverend John W. DeVilbiss found that out in 1846 in San Antonio. A circuit-riding Methodist preacher, the Ohio-born DeVilbiss figured there was plenty of work for him when he arrived in the new republic in December 1842. In fact, someone had warned him not to drink any water from the Sabine when he crossed into Texas, "as it gave a person an inclination to steal." Like other pioneer Texas preachers, DeVilbiss traveled from one community to another, dodging hostile Native Americans and trying to redirect the inclinations of Texans who had drunk from the Sabine.

When DeVilbiss conducted a camp meeting on McCoy's Creek, a tributary of the Guadalupe near present-day Cuero in South Texas, a detachment of Captain Jack Hay's Texas Rangers stood guard. The Rangers impressed the preacher. Like most of the early men of the cloth who came to Texas, DeVilbiss was a writer as well as an orator. He sent letters to the *Western Christian Advocate* from time to time with observations of his new home country. In one of those dispatches, he wrote about the Rangers.

By this time, he had settled near San Antonio, where he preached and started a Sunday school. Though some San Antonians were pleased with the opportunity to learn more about the Bible, Sunday school started at the same time of day as the weekly cockfight. Large crowds gathered for these rooster matches, and in addition to reducing the attendance of his missionary efforts, they made a lot of noise.

As if that were not enough for a preacher to worry about, a rumor got out that DeVilbiss had written some unflattering things about the Rangers. Some of Hay's Rangers, having stood guard while DeVilbiss sought converts, found it annoying that he would write something unfavorable about them. Of course, they hadn't read the story. They were merely depending on rumor.

Word reached the preacher that a group of six Rangers planned to "duck" him on Saturday night. (Accounts of this incident don't explain exactly what "duck" meant in this particular context, but it might have had something to do with immersion in the San Antonio River.) DeVilbiss sent a messenger to tell the offended Rangers that if they would delay their planned visit with him until Sunday morning, when they were welcome at his service, he would explain the perceived insult. The Rangers postponed the ducking, came to hear him preach and were satisfied with his explanation of the writing in question.

It turned out that a number of the Rangers had previously been regulars at the standing Sabbath cockfight, but they were so impressed by DeVilbiss's oratory that they started coming to his church instead. Attendance eventually dropped off so much the chicken fighting stopped—for the time being.

In 1859, while out for a Sabbath stroll, San Antonio visitor Edward E. Cross happened to be walking past a Catholic church when he noticed two Mexican men kneeling reverently near the door. Given that mass was being celebrated inside, that would have been perfectly understandable, except for one puzzling thing. Each man held what Cross called a "smart gamecock" under his arm. "Pious souls!" he later wrote. "They had evidently paused a moment on their way to the cockpit in order to brush over their little shortcomings for the past week."

"Mexican amusements, in the shape of cockfights and fandangoes, help to elevate and refine the people of San Antonio, such as choose to participate," Cross continued. "Every Sunday, just after mass at the old Mission Church [the Alamo Chapel], there is a cockfight, generally numerously attended. The pit is located in the rear of the church, about one square distant."

The fact that San Antonio residents participated in the blood sport of pitting one fighting chicken against the other was new to Cross when he visited in 1859, but it was not new to San Antonio.

When U.S. Army lieutenant Zebulon Pike arrived in San Antonio in 1807, it was still a remote Spanish colonial settlement; he carefully observed the residents and their culture. In his 1810 report of his explorations of areas west of the Mississippi, he devoted a few lines to the favorite "amusements"

For generations, cockfighting was a popular "sport" in the Alamo City. *Author's collection.*

of Bejarinos, including their penchant for gambling. "Their games are cards, billiards, horse racing and cockfighting, the first and last of which are carried to the most extravagant lengths, losing and winning immense sums."

The *San Antonio Express* expounded on—and denounced—cockfighting in its January 9, 1885 issue: "Any Sunday afternoon, if you go across San Pedro Creek into the Mexican quarters, you will come to a corner where the shrill crowing of roosters and the subdued hum of voices attracts your attention. Entering a saloon and paying a ten-cents toll at the back door, you are admitted into the cockpit." The pit, the newspaper continued, was generally sixteen feet across, surrounded by seats. Inside the pit would be two groups of men, each supporting or betting on a rooster whose scaly spurs had been further weaponized with attached sharp blades about three inches long.

"You hear the clink of money and the settling of bets. Then all is ready, and the crowd clears the pit and ascending the seats watches with eager eyes. The principals then get their birds in fighting condition by harassing them with side roosters, pulling feathers from their shields, et cetera. Then each holds his forward for a preliminary peck at its opponent." The holder of each bird then removes the leather sheaths from the blades on his rooster and tosses it into the ring opposite its opponent. "One or two quick flaps suffice, and one of them, bleeding and limp, is thrown out upon the spoliatum, and the pit again is filled with those making up the next fight."

The newspaper piece ended with a mini sermon: "The excitement at the cockpit is upon the part of horror and is improper, while the moral effect cannot but be attended with evil results. The law in most states is very strict upon this game, and it is to be hoped that it will not be long tolerated in Texas."

Despite the newspaper's desire to end to cockfighting in San Antonio, on May 1, 1885, the *El Paso Times* reported that "not long ago, there were a series of cockfights in San Antonio, some of which took place on Sundays, and they were all attended by the mayor, aldermen and the leading citizens of the Alamo City."

Though cockfighting did become less obvious to the general public, the blood sport continued on a more discreet level well into the twentieth century. "San Antonio has the fiercest breed of chickens on Earth," iconoclastic editor John S. Bonner wrote in the February 1910 issue of his monthly magazine, the *Harpoon*. "At the last cockfight reported from the hot tamale metropolis, one man was killed, and another lost one arm. Those San Antonio roosters are half a lap ahead of Austin's soft glove boxers."

That spring, the April 6 edition of the *Express* noted that testimony in a recent murder trial indicated that a cockpit had been operating "undisturbed" for several months. "It may be the police could not find it and then it may be they were attending the cockfights," the newspaper observed.

Frank Bushick, in his *Glamorous Days of Old San Antonio*, recalled that the Western Star Saloon had a pit behind it that was nearly always surrounded by betters and onlookers. "Many a poor chanticleer fought to an untimely end to make a Roman holiday for a motley crowd resembling grand opera villains or a battalion of Pancho Villa's army," he wrote.

According to a vintage visitor-oriented publication from 1911, the Alamo City had two flourishing cockpits, the Monterrey at 302 South Santa Rosa and the nearby Ogden's Cock Pit at 225 South Santa Rosa. Both places had fights starting at 8:00 p.m. on Saturdays and, in deference to the church crowd, at 2:00 p.m. on Sundays. Admission to both places cost fifteen cents.

Old customs die as hard as a well-bred fighting rooster. On Sunday, August 30, 2020, Bexar County sheriff's deputies broke up a cockfight in the southeastern part of the county, making three arrests and issuing twenty-one

Though long since illegal, betting on roosters with razor-sharp spurs still occurs. *Mike Cox photograph.*

citations. Deputies found a supply of trophies intended for owners whose birds survived and assorted cockfighting paraphernalia. They confiscated fifty-two roosters and handed them over to county animal control officers, who also disposed of six dead roosters found at the scene.

16

MR. BEAN, LATE OF BEANVILLE

Before the bearded, big-bellied, red-faced scalawag later known as Judge Roy Bean became famous as the "Law West of the Pecos," he was just another scoundrel in San Antonio.

Born Phantly Roy Bean in Kentucky in 1835, he left home as a teenager to travel with an older brother to the California gold fields. On their way west, they passed through San Antonio, and after several years on the Pacific coast, he became a teamster on the Chihuahua Trail, hauling goods via San Antonio to Mexico.

When the Civil War broke out, Bean made money hauling cotton to Mexico to circumvent the Union blockade. After the war, in the fall of 1866, he married eighteen-year-old Maria Anastacia Virginia Chavez (some sources say she was only fifteen or sixteen years old at the time), who came from a prominent family whose presence in San Antonio traced to the arrival of a group of colonists from the Canary Islands in 1731.

While he had married into a landed family, Bean still had to make a living. Whether it was an honest living did not seem to matter. His first non-freight hauling enterprise involved providing wood to feed the furnaces of a local ironworks. He also sold firewood to others. Not having land of his own to harvest, he became creative when coming up with fuel.

His supply chain came under scrutiny, and on April 18, 1875, a Bexar County grand jury indicted him for swindling. Specifically, the indictment alleged that Bean had charged one Francisco Andsada ten dollars (which was a considerable sum at the time) for the right to gather wood "on the left side of the Garza Road, when in truth and in fact, he, the said Roy Bean, did not own any land or wood on the left side of the Garza Road." The charge was soon dismissed when the district attorney became persuaded of Bean's innocence after reading a sworn statement alleging that the complaining witness against Bean had only been trying to cover up the fact that he had stolen the wood from someone else. Whether that was actually the case or if it was the work of a creative defense attorney employed in Bean's behalf is a matter of speculation.

Bean faced more serious legal troubles in the summer of 1878, when the *Galveston News* correspondent in San Antonio reported that Bean had been arrested the night of August 13 "for making an assault on a Mexican named Martinez." The short item also noted that Bean had been intoxicated.

While Bean preferred the stronger stuff, he thought he might be able to make a living selling milk. The manner in which he obtained his herd proved questionable, and his milk cows were so poor that they could barely produce. Still, he managed to provide his customers with what old-time Texans called sweet milk. But this enterprise dried up when a local judge found a minnow swimming in his milk. When confronting the vendor, the irate jurist accused Bean of diluting his product with river water. Feigning shock, Bean said something like, "Well, I'll be damned. One of my cows must have swallowed that minnow when she drank at the river."

Early in their marriage, the Beans lived about a mile south of town off the road to Corpus Christi on land owned by Maria's family. After Bean was able to accumulate a little money, he moved his family to their own place. According to the *San Antonio Light*, the area, now the 400 block of Glenn Avenue, became known as Beanville "from the fact that it was largely through his enterprise that the property was subdivided and sold in town lots."

Despite his questionable business practices, heavy drinking and penchant for violence, Bean seems to have been an affable sort who could tell a good story. As a devoted husband, however, he fell a bit short. He and Maria would have four children and adopt a fifth, but they did not have a pacific marriage. When Bean beat Maria and burned her with a chunk of wood pulled from their fireplace, she filed charges against him. But during the trial, when asked by the judge to show the scars she alleged that her husband had left her with, she refused, believing it immodest. Lacking any tangible evidence of an assault, the judge dismissed the case. But when Maria went to the court to sue for divorce, her petition was granted. That occurred in 1881, and by the summer, Bean had sold his house and left town to sell beer and whiskey to the thousands of workers who were then laying track for the nation's second transcontinental railroad.

Before he became the "Law West of the Pecos" in Langtry, Texas, Roy Bean lived for nearly two decades in San Antonio. *Postcard from author's collection.*

While doing research on Bean's time in San Antonio, longtime *San Antonio Express* reporter John MacCormack found the draft of an article in the files of the San Antonio Conservation Society that suggests Bean's move westward was not entirely his idea. "After his seventeen years' residence here and [various] misdemeanors and a vast accumulation of debts, the city fathers ran him out of town, as they expressed it 'for the good of the town,'" the unnamed author wrote.

If the move was good for San Antonio, it proved even better for Bean. Two hundred miles to the west, Bean opened a saloon at a railroad stop named Langtry. He also provided travelers meals and sundries. Not long after, there being an extremely limited pool of prospects, the commissioner's court of the newly created Val Verde County named Bean justice of the peace.

Thanks to the steady flow of traffic on the newly completed east–west mainline, passengers who alighted from the train for a meal and a drink or two at Bean's modest establishment began spreading the stories they heard of the judge's antics. Soon, reporters passing through Langtry started writing about the eccentric proprietor who, while being only modestly educated, was clearly smart enough to understand that what today would be called "news media exposure" was good for business. It being the height of the so-called yellow journalism era, a time when the relevancy of truth sank to a new low, Roy Bean became a legend in his own lifetime.

It's not that Bean did not pull off some outlandish things in his dual capacity as saloon keeper and justice of the peace, but they got magnified with each retelling. Even so, it does seem to be true that while fulfilling his statutory duties as coroner, he did rule a dead man guilty of illegally carrying a pistol and fined him forty dollars—the exact amount of cash he happened to have on his body. And at an examining trial, the judge refused to allow a murder charge to move forward against a trigger-happy cowboy who had killed a Chinese railroad worker, declaring that he could find nothing in state statutes that said it was illegal to murder an Asian in Texas.

The judge definitely had his own view of what constituted justice, as well as a good sense of humor. He also had a pet black bear that someone had captured in the area. Bean had grown particularly fond of the animal, which he unimaginatively named Bruno. In truth, Bruno was more of a business partner than a pet. And like Bean, he had a taste for cold beer. People from

Bean as depicted in an early newspaper sketch. *Author's collection.*

the East thought that quite amusing and were generally happy to stand Bruno a brew just to watch him down a bottle and perform some of the tricks Bean had taught him. That suited Bruno just fine, and of course, it added nicely to his owner's daily receipts.

Bean never again lived in San Antonio, but since it was less than a four-hour train ride to the east, he periodically returned for business or personal reasons. Often, he'd go on an extended toot while catching up with old friends and taking in a cockfight or two. On one of those visits, the noted practical joker got the tables turned on him in a particularly cruel way.

The judge was holding nonjudicial court in one of the Alamo City's many saloons when a traveling salesman recognized him and came up to note that he'd recently passed through Langtry. "Did you see my bear?" the judge asked. "I should say I did," the drummer replied. "I saw him uncork a bottle of beer and drink it, and I was there when he died." Overwhelmed with grief, the old judge dismissed the salesman and ruminated over the loss of Bruno. After a few more drinks, it occurred to Bean that a way existed for him to hang on to his late pet, at least in a sense. He left for the telegraph office, where he wired his loyal factotum. "Skin bear and ship hide by express to me at once. I want to have it stuffed." When a few hours later a messenger delivered Bean a reply to his wire, the judge read it and began cursing in rage: "Bear hated to die, and I sure hated shooting him. Skin shipped to you by express as ordered."

By the time of his death in the spring of 1903, Bean had become one of the Old West's better-known figures. Newspapers in the Alamo City overlooked the judge's moral and ethical failings and instead portrayed him as a principled eccentric. "Bean was not what is known as a 'bad' man," one of the newspapers said in reporting his passing. "On the contrary, he had a scrupulous regard for the right as he saw it. He had a great contempt for the finesse of lawyers, and generally rode roughshod over all technicalities and rendered such judgment as he thought was right." Observing that Bean's death "removes another of the pioneers and old Indian fighters of West Texas," the newspaper eulogized him as "a man of strict integrity and honesty." Presumably setting down those words with a straight face, the anonymous journalist concluded, "He was not polished, but from beneath his rough coating, there was emitted the sparkle of the gem under it."

17

THE STORY THE OLD SHERIFF TOLD

As a lawman, Thomas M. Stell had once jailed John Wesley Hardin, one of the Wild West's most feared gunmen. But when reflecting on his career years later, it was the backstory of what began as a "routine" shooting involving a San Antonio police officer that he saw as considerably more interesting than his dealings with Hardin.

The eighty-three-year-old Stell, who served as De Witt County sheriff from 1892 to 1906, related the story in a letter he sent to *Frontier Times* magazine publisher J. Marvin Hunter in the spring of 1939. "I had a fall on the thirteenth of January, in which I sustained a broken hip—a serious condition for a man eighty-three years old—and I am very slowly recovering from the effects," Stell began. "After five months of suffering, I can hobble around on crutches," he continued. "The shock and pain shattered my nerves to such an extent that I can scarcely write my name, yet my memory is so aroused that I feel impelled to give expression to memories of scenes, incidents and personalities that loom in the panorama of the past."

One of those incidents occurred in San Antonio shortly after the turn of the twentieth century. Flo Williams, the keeper of what polite society referred to as a "notorious house"—a combination saloon, gambling house and bordello at Nuevo and Laredo Streets in the Alamo City—was no candidate for a nunnery, but she wanted to keep her place as respectable as possible. Allowing hardcases to hang around was bad for business.

Considering her line of work, Flo knew a lot of people, but she'd never seen the heavy-set, tough-looking man who walked into her place around midnight on April 16, 1902. He didn't have much to say at first, but as he continued to knock down drinks, he became increasingly more garrulous. Disingenuously bragging that he was an outlaw, he said he'd recently done an eight-year stretch in prison and had killed several men during the course of his career as a badman. Just in case Flo and others in the saloon didn't believe him, he opened his coat to reveal that he was carrying a revolver. At that, Flo discreetly told one of her girls to call the police.

Three mounted officers, Pink Taylor, Frank Harvey and D.E. Hughes, arrived about 2:30 a.m. Flo told the officers the suspicious character was sitting at one of the tables in a back room. When they entered the room, before the uniformed officers could say a word, a man jumped up, jerked out a concealed six-shooter and fired a shot at them. What felt like a gut punch sent Officer Harvey reeling backward, but when he looked down, expecting to see blood, there was none. The bullet had hit his belt buckle, a piece of brass sufficiently strong enough to keep the slug from penetrating his abdomen. The buckle had been ruined, but not him.

In the same instant, the two other officers rushed the shooter in an attempt to disarm him, but when he kept trying to get off another shot, Officer Taylor pulled his revolver and put three bullets in the man. He died almost immediately, never having said a word.

That's the way the newspapers described what happened that morning, but Stell's version is a bit different. He didn't say so, but if the shooting went down like he said, it had happened the second time officers had come in contact with the man, not the first.

Stell said the man had rented a room at a boardinghouse and that his demeanor had gotten the attention of his landlady. She told police that the stranger kept a low profile, never speaking with any of the other boarders. And he never left his room during the day, only venturing forth for an hour or two after supper. Usually returning by 9:00 or 10:00 p.m., he'd head straight for his room. Whoever he was, he kept up with current events, always returning with copies of that day's newspapers.

While her tenant's lone-wolf nature was really none of her business, the landlady grew suspicious that he was a criminal on the dodge and notified police. As Stell recalled, "The officers…concluded they would go that evening about supper time…[and] interrogate him." But when officers arrived on the evening of April 15, they found that the man in question had already eaten and "gone out into the city." With no probable cause and no search warrant, the officers got the landlady to let them into his room. The only thing of interest they found was a box of .45-caliber cartridges but no weapon. While that was suspicious, it was not necessarily incriminating. Still, they wanted to question the man, so they waited until he came back to his room.

When the man walked into the boardinghouse, Stell said "the three officers rose up as one…[but] even before they had spoken a word, [he] surmised they were officers, and I think he supposed that they were cognizant of his identity." Actually, the officers did not know who he was, "but they were sure of one thing, that he was a desperado and badly wanted somewhere." It seems more likely, however, that the officers told their informant to call the station when the man returned and then left to continue making their rounds.

However the shooting went down, the dead man had no identification on him. The next day, a reporter for the *San Antonio Light* who had gone to view the body at the undertaker's found the name Wyatt Hanks stitched under the collar of the dead man's tailor-made coat. Police did not know of any local characters by that name, but someone with the department remembered that a man named Camilla Hanks was wanted in Montana for train robbery and murder. Bexar County sheriff John W. Tobin wired authorities there and learned that Camilla Hanks was well known to them, a cowboy originally from the Cuero, Texas area who had gone very bad. Still, San Antonio officers did not know if the man Officer Taylor had killed was Camilla Hanks

A profile of Hanks prepared by the Pinkerton National Detective Agency listed his nickname and alias ("Deaf Charley" and "Charlie Jones") and noted that he had served time in the Deer Lodge, Montana's state prison, for a train robbery committed near Big Timber, Montana, in 1892. Released from the penitentiary in April 1901, after serving eight years of a ten-year sentence, he had demonstrated the extent of his rehabilitation by taking part in the robbery of a Great Northern Railroad train on July 3, 1910. Two trainmen had been shot in the holdup, one fatally. One of the passengers had also been wounded in the holdup, a crime which netted the bandits some $65,000 in unsigned bank notes. It was the final crime attributed to one of the Old West's most notorious gangs, the Wild Bunch. "Low-browed, mastiff-jawed and bull necked," the profile said, "[Camilla] Hanks enjoys the distinction of being the most bestial and truculent scoundrel among his many noted criminal colleagues."

Meanwhile, investigators learned that Wyatt Hanks was the brother of the wanted man and was still alive. Now pretty sure that the dead man was Camilla Hanks, Sheriff Tobin needed absolute confirmation. That's when he

A contemporary newspaper engraving of Wild Bunch gang member Camilla "Deaf Charlie" Hanks made from his prison photograph. *Author's collection.*

contacted Stell, who told his law enforcement colleague that he had known Hanks since childhood. It had been seventeen or eighteen years since he'd seen him, Stell continued, but "unless he had changed very materially, I would certainly recognize him." To back him up, Stell contacted a first cousin of Hanks, and the two traveled by train the eighty miles between Cuero and San Antonio.

At the morgue, Stell and Hanks's cousin positively identified the dead man as Camilla Hanks. "It was a very unpleasant situation for me as I gazed on the face of the dead man and recognized him as a boyhood friend and schoolmate…but my duty as an officer compelled me to voice recognition," the old lawman wrote. "It was still more unpleasant for his cousin to give his assent to the recognition, and he refused to have anything more to do with the affair."

Hanks, a distant descendant of Abraham Lincoln's mother, Nancy Hanks, was born in Dewitt County around 1863. His grandfather had been one of Stephen F. Austin's original three hundred colonists in Texas. "I…can truthfully say that on his mother's side, he came from one of the finest families in the area," Stell said. "I never knew what disposition was made of the body.…But this I do know, that while he died the ignominious death of an outlaw, he had as fine a heritage bequeathed to him as ever fell to the lot of any mortal."

His identity confirmed, Hanks was buried at the county's expense in City Cemetery No. 4 on East Commerce Street.

At the conclusion of his letter, Stell told Hunter that he had not thought about the incident for years until a recent "write up" on Butch Cassidy and the Wild Bunch had triggered the memory. "It set me to musing but, as I said…my recollection of [Hank's] death has no historical value or interest except to myself." Fortunately, Hunter disagreed with the old-timer's judgment in that regard and published Stell's letter. Only a few months later, Stell died on July 3.

18

"WHERE LIFE IS LIVELY"

The man standing in front of the gambling establishment puffed on a San Antonio–made Maverick cigar with an air of perfect contentment. A reporter recognized him as Lee Cotton, one of the Alamo City's better known professional gamblers. "Hello, Lee! What are you doing now?" the journalist called out.

"Who, me? I'm in jail."

"Don't say! How long you been in?"

"Oh, I dunno."

Looking to Dick Strayhorn, another well-known "notorious all-round sport," Cotton asked: "Hey, Dick, how long have I been in jail?"

Dick thought on that for a minute. "'Bout a week, Lee, ain't it?"

"Yes, I guess so. Anyhow, I know the time's up next Wednesday."

"How do you work it, Lee?" the reporter asked.

"Why, I just drive out to the poorhouse every night at 6 o'clock and report," Cotton said. "Then I come back to town till the same hour next evening."

Cotton had been sentenced to jail for conducting a gambling operation. But an understanding judge, perhaps one of the many patrons of San Antonio's so-called Sporting District, had been willing to temper justice and allow Cotton to serve his three-week imprisonment for five minutes a day. "After having reported to the keeper of the poorhouse at 6 o'clock," the journalist explained, "in the evening [Cotton] was free to return to the city and deal faro until 5 or 6 o'clock in the morning."

Left: When found guilty of practicing his trade, Alamo City gambler Lee Cotton couldn't kick about his sentence. *Author's collection.*

Below: San Antonio remained the "Las Vegas" of South Texas well into the twentieth century. *Postcard from author's collection.*

With some fifty thousand residents, San Antonio reigned as the largest city in Texas. Of that population, the journalist noted, at least five hundred—or 1 percent of the entire city—made their living as gamblers. Sometimes, the reporter continued, as many as eight hundred Knights of the Green Cloth plied their trade in the Alamo City. "Gambling is the only vice which is not licensed directly in San Antonio," the journalist explained. "The games are run openly, and the gamblers are 'fined' two or three times a year. They also have to 'go to jail' about as often."

The article continued, "Nobody ever thinks of going to bed in San Antonio before midnight, and the number of persons who turn night into day is greater in proportion than in any other place in the Union. Saloons and restaurants there are by scores that never close their doors from year's end to another, and variety theaters and dance halls are in full blast at night."

The best-known and most elegant of the gaming houses was the White Elephant, opened in 1883. For visitors, it rivaled the Alamo in popularity. "Art and Sybaritic luxury served to make the surroundings attractive," wrote Frank Bushick in his *Glamorous Days*. "[The] opening night reception was attended by many people of the city of both sexes. Giggle water and edibles of the most expensive character…were lavishly dispensed without money and without price. Everything was on the house."

Other noted venues included the 101, the Arlington, the Fashion, the Ranch, the Revolving Light and the Silver King. The journalist who illustrated how the local criminal justice system viewed gaming stressed that gambling in the Alamo City was "conducted in an orderly, quiet, businesslike way, and rows or fights very seldom occur." Then he explained one of the reasons that was so:

> *In the cash drawer of every faro, roulette, monte or poker table lies a little machine which lets out a bit of cold lead at the same time that it lets a man's soul out of his body. The gentlemen who preside behind these tables are of cool temperament, gentle of speech and courteous in manner, but when their fingers are dallying with the trigger of a six-shooter they are apt to be dangerous.*

The only inaccuracy in that paragraph was the reporter's characterization of a just-fired bullet as being cold. Back on target in his reporting, the writer—clearly no stranger to smoke-filled gaming establishments—painted this picture of professional gamblers in the Alamo City: "[They] are the best-dressed men in the town. Most of their clothes come from New York and are made to order by Broadway tailors. They give more to charity than any other class. They are esteemed citizens, and while they do not mingle in the more exclusive circles of society, their friendship is sought after by the solid merchants of the town."

As for who availed themselves of opportunities to wager on games of chance in the sporting district, "The games are supported by cattlemen, ranchmen, a few inveterate city 'pikers' and by tourists. The cattlemen and ranchmen quite often win large sums of money; the 'pikers' pick up a scanty living at the game, but the tourists almost invariably lose, although the games are square."

The author concluded his piece by opining that in San Antonio, gambling was merely an "eccentricity," not an activity deemed as injurious to the public. The attitude that gambling was good for the local economy continued for decades after this story appeared in newspapers.

Occasionally, for political reasons, police would raid a gambling joint. On the last day of February 1883, the Alamo City's finest asserted their authority. The March 1 edition of the *San Antonio Light*, under a three-deck headline beginning with "Teasing the Tiger," covered one of those short-lived crackdowns:

> *Last night, the police decided to make a raid upon the gamblers and proposed at first to make a simultaneous raid upon all the prominent gambling dens in the city. Unfortunately, this was impossible by reason of the limited force, and ultimately it was decided to make a raid upon the two nearest gambling saloons to the police station, those known by the name of Arlington and the Green Front.*

Virtually the entire police force, one squad for each of the gambling joints, rushed into the front and back doors of their target venues at 10:00 p.m. "No sooner was the whistle sounded than the police rushed in…and took their station at the tables," the *Light* continued. "Had a cannon ball fallen into the room, it could not have created greater consternation. At the tables were some of the most noted gamblers in the city, and before them were the piles of dollars so fascinating to the victims of the infatuating pastime."

The dealers, those sweating the games and some of the players were arrested and marched to the hoosegow. The proprietors covered the dealers' bonds and paid the twenty-dollar fine assessed the players, but no further mention of the raids appeared in the *Light*, and soon it was business as usual at both places.

Not until 1941, shortly before the United States entered the Second World War, did a colonel then stationed at Fort Sam Houston succeed in getting city officials to shut down the Sporting District by making it off-limits to military personnel. His name was Dwight D. Eisenhower, future supreme Allied commander and later president.

After the war, the Sporting District did not come back to life. But even then, to place money on the belief that organized gambling had ended in the Alamo City was a sucker's bet.

19
THE LETTER OF THE LAW

At the beginning of the twentieth century, San Antonio was Texas's largest city. Like all cities, its local government enacted both civil and criminal ordinances aimed at making it a safe and livable community. The first set of ordinances had been adopted with the incorporation of the city in 1870. Twenty-nine years later, the city fathers approved a revised body of ordinances. Violating any of them constituted a misdemeanor.

How strictly the city marshal, a job title later changed to chief of police, chose to enforce these ordinances varied from administration to administration, but the ordinances on the books gave officers a wide range of arrest options. For instance, if a cowboy rode to town from a nearby ranch, it was illegal to hitch or tie "any horse, mule, jack, jennet or other animal on Main Avenue between Main Plaza and Veramendi Street."

Speaking of four-footed modes of transportation:

> *Any person or persons who shall lead or ride, or cause to be ridden, any horse, mule or any other animal, or any person or persons who shall drive, or cause to be driven, any carriage, wagon, cart, dray or any other vehicle drawn by animals, or shall ride any bicycle, across or upon any sidewalk, shall be fined in any sum not less than one dollar ($1.00) nor more than ten dollars ($10.00) for each and every offence; provided, that the crossing of a sidewalk by a person so riding or driving for the purpose of entering upon private premises, shall not be construed as a violation of this ordinance.*

San Antonio City Hall, where local ordinances have been enacted and offenders adjudicated since its opening in 1891. *Postcard from author's collection.*

You've heard the expression, "No bull!" Well, that was definitely the case in the Alamo City, where, "It shall be unlawful for the owner, agent or person having in charge any bull over one year of age, to permit such bull to run at large in any portion of the city limits." So much for San Antonio ever adopting Spain's annual running of the bulls.

It was also an offense for anyone to "ride or drive any wild horses or other wild animal in or through the streets, alleys or plazas of this city."

The ordinances also covered the matter of livestock ownership. There's nothing like a well-cooked slice of ham or bacon with your eggs, but the animals that provided those two protein sources could not be kept too close to the city. One ordinance declared it a nuisance to keep "a hog or hogs in a pen or enclosure within the city limits on the north, two and a half miles, on the east, two and a half miles on the south, and to [the] corporation line on the west as far south as…Grenada Street, and thence one mile on the west of the cupola of the cathedral of San Francisco."

For generations, San Antonio had been known for its fandangos, or lively public dances. But in Victorian times, not so much. The 1899 ordinances mandated, "All public balls in this city shall be unlawful, unless by permit from the mayor; every public ball shall be attended during the whole time thereof by at least one policeman."

When Jim Bowie died at the Alamo, in his final moments, having discharged his brace of pistols, he may have grabbed the wicked knife that bore his name. But that was in 1836. In civilized San Antonio, carrying a Bowie knife was specifically prohibited by the 1899 ordnance, as was the carrying of other deadly weapons:

> *If any person within the corporate limits of the city of San Antonio, shall carry on or about his or her person, saddle or in his saddle bags, any pistol, dirk, dagger, sling shot, sword cane, spear or knuckles made of any metal or any hard substance, Bowie knife or any other kind of knife manufactured or sold for purposes of offense or defense, he or she shall be punished by a fine of not less than twenty-five dollars ($25.00) nor more than two hundred dollars ($200.00).*
>
> *The preceding shall not apply…to the carrying of arms on one's own premises or place of business, nor to persons traveling, nor to one who has a reasonable ground for fearing an unlawful attack upon his person.*

Twenty-first-century San Antonio still has some quirky statutes on the books. For instance, under chapter 21, "Offenses and Miscellaneous Provisions," it is illegal to climb pecan trees in public parks or to throw sticks, stones or "other missiles for the purpose of gathering pecans." Other no-no's elsewhere in the city code include hurling or throwing anything from the Tower of the Americas observation deck; parachuting from the Tower of the Americas; spitting on the sidewalk (or the floors of churches, public halls, theaters, motor buses "or other similar public place") and flirting or reacting to flirtation "with eyes or hands."

20

A COWBOY FOR TO BE

Sam Bass was born in Indiana, it was his native home,
And at the age of seventeen, young Sam began to roam.
Sam first came out to Texas a cowboy for to be.

—Nineteenth-century folk ballad based on the short life of the notorious outlaw Sam Bass, killed by Texas Rangers in 1878

Already a decade into the twentieth century, Texas and the rest of the nation was modernizing at a rapid pace. Automobiles were soon to become more common than horses and buggies, the army in San Antonio was experimenting with flying machines and Morse code messages could be sent through the air via wireless telegraphy to ships far at sea. But one thing had not changed by 1910: the nation's fascination with the supposedly romantic life of the western cowboy.

William F. "Buffalo Bill" Cody's Wild West Show had gone a long way toward mythologizing the cowboy, and now the nascent movie industry was adding to the public's perception that wrangling cattle was a more glamorous way to earn a living than working on a farm, in a factory or in retail. Indeed, the cowboy had become such a popular cultural figure that the Texas governor's office and postmasters across the state regularly received letters from out-of-state women wanting the names of marriageable wranglers.

One person who understood America's fascination with cowboying was an Illinois man who likely never came any closer to a cow than a ribeye steak. Harry A. Smith had been saddled with a decidedly ordinary surname, but he proved to be a gifted grifter who came up with a new twist to an old con.

Newly arrived in the bustling Alamo City, Smith (also known as Carl Smith) was making several hundred dollars daily by offering adventure-minded northerners an opportunity to come to the Lone Star State, "a cowboy for to be." Smith's investment had been minimal. He rented a small downtown office and placed advertisements in Chicago newspapers seeking men who'd like a cowboying job on a large South Texas spread not far from San Antonio, the "Great Rincon Ranch." New hires would be paid forty dollars a month, live in a comfortable bunkhouse and be fed good grub. But the Rincon was not looking for just another stove-up waddie. What ranch management sought for the sprawling Rincon were "energetic, strong young men, different from the old-fashioned Texas cowboy." For more details, anyone interested in coming to Texas to begin enjoying a life of unfettered freedom on the wide-open plains was encouraged to write Smith in San Antonio. Those who did received this printed letter:

> *Dear Sir: Yours of* [the date] *at hand and upon your immediate acceptance I grant you a position on the Rincon ranch as cowboy. Now, to make it more easy* [sic] *for you, I will make this offer. If you pay your car fare* [as in railroad car] *from Chicago, it will cost you about $30. This is our plan to those who cannot afford that amount at present. If upon acceptance of the position you enclose $2, we will send you a first-class railway ticket, good from Chicago to San Antonio, the balance to be taken out of your salary at the rate of $5 per month, and if you are with us six months, we return this money to you. But of course, if you have the ready money, you can pay your fare if it suits you best.*

But wait, as product pitchers like to say, there was more. "Now about the job. We pay you forty dollars per month and furnish room and board and also saddle horse and complete outfit."

However, the job was only for men willing to live up to the cowboy code. "We do not want any rowdies or drunkards," the form letter continued.

> *That is why we are breaking in city boys. We devote the first few days to getting you used to the saddle and the art of throwing a rope. I am sure you will not regret having joined us once you get acquainted with the boys.*

> *Now, one word more. Immediately upon your acceptance I will send you all necessary instructions regarding the day of leaving, et cetera. Answer as soon as possible.*
> *Very truly,*
> *CARL SMITH, 209 Soledad Street, San Antonio, Texas*

Oh, and P.S., "If you have a couple of friends who would like to join us, please show them this letter."

For two heady weeks after his advertisements began appearing, each day's mail brought Smith dozens of letters containing two dollars. To put that in perspective, in 1910, a couple of dollars had the equivalent buying power of nearly sixty dollars today. In other words, the nation's infatuation with cowboys was bringing the huckster a lot of easy "mailbox" money.

Unfortunately for the enterprising "cowboy factory" agent, someone who sent in two dollars but heard nothing more from Smith realized he'd been taken and reported the matter to a postal inspector. Clearly, Smith was using the U.S. mail for fraudulent purposes. After a San Antonio–based postal inspector determined there was no such place as the Rincon Ranch, a warrant charging Smith with mail fraud was served by U.S. marshal Thomas Holloman on the evening of November 19.

In Smith's downtown office, investigators confiscated hundreds of dollars and a supply of his fraudulent form letters. Booked into the Bexar County Jail, Smith was being held in lieu of a $2,000 bond. Newspapers noted that despite his alleged windfall from his "cowboy factory" scheme, Smith didn't have enough money to handle his bail.

Even as Smith had sought to cash in on the national fascination with Texas cowpokes, one newspaper noted, "While the cowboy is still an institution in Southwest Texas, he has practically disappeared from the vicinity of San Antonio, the cutting up of the large cattle ranches into farms, relegating him to the pages of fiction or history, or driving him to the still remaining large ranches in Northwest Texas."

On January 3, 1911, Smith entered a plea of guilty to the mail fraud charge and U.S. district judge Thomas S. Maxey sentenced him to six months in the county jail. Whether he got credit for time already served was not reported.

Life behind bars was sweet for Smith—literally. The *San Antonio Light* reported on March 15, 1911, that two or three times a week, the prisoner's mother and sister in Danville, Illinois, were sending the convicted scam artist boxes of homemade candy. The very U.S. mail that the prisoner had used

Long since razed, this is the post office and federal courthouse where "cowboy factory" scam artist Harry A. Smith pleaded guilty to postal fraud. *Postcard from author's collection.*

to bilk money from others also brought him a steady supply of magazines and newspapers to help him while away his time in the clink. "Cellmates of Smith enjoy a feast every time the box of [candy] arrives," the newspaper noted. "Good naturedly, he distributes them, passing some from cell to cell."

Given his common last name, beyond the fact that he had relatives in Illinois, little is known of Smith's background other than he must have been reasonably well educated and possessed of a creative mindset. He may have been the Harry A. Smith who, in early 1910, served as the private secretary and "handy boy" of Chicago mayor Fred Busse until the *Chicago Inter Ocean* exposed corrupt practices on the part of his honor, the mayor, Smith and others in Busse's administration. But the mayor was never prosecuted and apparently neither was Smith. If the Smith who dodged a legal bullet in Chicago was the same person who ran the cowboy scam in San Antonio, it may have been the adverse publicity he received in the Windy City that inspired him to leave for Texas.

What became of Smith after he completed his sentence has not been determined. But it may be that he lived less than a decade after his release from the Bexar County Jail. The name "Harry A. Smith" is carved on a monument in Danville, Illinois, honoring local soldiers who died in World War I.

21

ADIOS, OLD GIBBET

It had a good run, thirty-two years. But sooner or later, all things must come to an end. Old Gibbet would soon be no more. "Old Gibbet" was the nickname of the gallows—also known as a gibbet—inside the Bexar County jail. Ten men had climbed its decidedly unlucky thirteen steps since its construction in 1878, but on October 2, 1910, the *San Antonio Light and Gazette* reported that Bexar County commissioners had decided to have the old scaffold torn down and replaced with a state-of-the-art hanging apparatus.

The *San Antonio Light and Gazette*, the afternoon daily newspaper, which, like most newspapers of the day, relished publishing detailed accounts of hangings, devoted two-thirds of a page to the history of the doomed gallows and the men who had been "jerked to Jesus" beneath it. Beginning with the hanging of Joe Cordova in 1879 and ending with the execution of Doc Williams in 1908, three white men, three Mexican men and four Black men had met their fates on the gibbet. "With clergymen and prayer to nerve them for the ordeal of paying the law's extreme penalty, there have stood, with arms pinioned and the black cap adjusted, [10 men] waiting for the click of the rigger which shot them into eternity," the unnamed journalist wrote. "Never has there been a hitch in the proceedings, and death usually came swiftly."

One of the more sensational hangings was that of sixty-year-old Juan Rocha, who had been convicted of the January 16, 1901 killing of his employer, John Grimsinger. Since Rocha murdered Grimsinger because

Only one poor-quality newspaper image of Old Gibbet is known to exist, but the Bexar County gallows looked similar to this nineteenth-century gallows. The location where this photograph was taken is not known. *Postcard from author's collection.*

Mrs. Guadalupe Rodriquez Grimsinger told him to—saying she was tired of her husband—by all rights, she should have been executed along with him, but a jury gave her a life prison sentence instead. Rocha was hanged on August 2 that year.

The article also noted the unusual fact that 20 percent of the men hanged at the gallows were one-legged. Charles Ward, hanged on August 21, 1882, for sexually assaulting an eleven-year-old girl, was the first one-legged man hanged there. He stood on crutches until the trapdoor gave way beneath him. The second hanged one-legged man was James McCoy, who was executed on August 23, 1889, for the murder of Sheriff Charles McKinney in nearby La Salle County on December 26, 1886.

The scaffold had been built by a carpenter remembered only by his last name of McDowell to accommodate the hanging of six men convicted of murdering a doctor in DeWitt County. "He did a good job," the article continued, "but the six men were never hanged because the higher court reversed the findings of the lower, and on a new trial, the men came clear." But the once-scheduled multiple hanging had influenced the design of the gallows, which had a crossbeam and trapdoor wide enough to handle three men at a time. While the gallows' sturdy timbers were simple enough, the mechanism for releasing the trapdoor beneath the feet of the condemned was a bit more complicated.

The soon-to-be replaced gallows, the article continued, "is built so that the trap is held by a rope which passed to a circular drum. Pins keep the drum in place until the final moment. Then the pin comes out, the weight of the criminal combined with that of the trapdoor forces it to fall with a lumbering noise." To throw the trapdoor, the reporter went on, the executioner stands on the floor below.

The last person executed on the old gibbet was Doc Williams, a man who succumbed to temptation while selling watermelons. Rather than split the proceeds with his partner, Williams killed him. Since the victim would no longer need his watch, Williams took that, too. But when his partner's partially burned body was discovered, police were able to find witnesses who had seen Williams with him shortly before he disappeared. When the stolen watch was found at a pawn shop, police learned Williams had been the one who pawned it.

Unlike his predecessors on the gallows, Williams made a last-minute bid for freedom that had nothing to do with the filing of a court document seeking a stay of execution or commutation. He pretended to hang himself, only to bolt out of his cell when a jailer opened his cell door to check on him.

He ran through the jail's kitchen to the jail's courtyard, climbed the wall and leaped down. Unfortunately, the fall broke his leg, ending his desperate bid for freedom. A doctor placed his leg in the cast he still wore when he was escorted up the steps of the gallows on July 21, 1908.

The reporter concluded his nostalgic look at the old scaffold by noting that there were no pending death penalty cases in Bexar County at that time, meaning the next person in need of hanging would die on a more modern device. Not only would the county be getting new gallows, but Bexar County officials had earmarked $30,000 for a complete remodeling and expansion of the old jail. The new facility was opened for public inspection in May 1912. Built to then-modern sanitary standards, the new lockup ended up costing $60,000.

The new gallows was not nearly as foreboding as the one it replaced. In fact, it was hardly noticeable. As the *Light* explained on May 5 that year:

> *Unless pointed out to visitors, the gallows in the new jail would not be recognized. It is a radical departure from the accepted methods employed.*
>
> *On the north side of the building, in the ceiling of the third floor may be seen an iron ring. Directly beneath it is a steel platform flush with the floor. There is no scaffold, no stairs to mount, no grim reminders of any sort except the solitary ring in the ceiling.*

When used, however, "the new death trap is just as efficacious as any other. The condemned man stands on the metal platform. The rope is fastened to the ring in the ceiling. One single movement of a lever causes the platform to drop. The man falls through the floor. There is a drop of about nine feet. Below, on the second floor, are the doctors."

Nearly a decade passed before George McKinely Grace had the dubious honor of being the first man hanged since the retirement of Old Gibbet. He was executed on January 6, 1922—the last legal hanging in San Antonio. Beginning in 1923, the Texas prison system began handling executions, and Bexar County's state-of-the-art hanging system became a relic of a bygone era.

22
THE LADY AND HER VALISE

The fifty-something-year-old lady emerging from the *Texas Special*, like any self-respecting woman of her day, wore a long, dark dress and a large hat pinned to her hair. Clutched tightly in her hand was a worn cloth valise, a small piece of luggage then commonly called a grip. Helping her down from the train that hot June 13 afternoon was a handsome, well-dressed gentleman who looked at least twenty years her junior. The nature of their relationship was not evident to anyone who might have noticed their arrival, but clearly, they had been traveling together.

Nothing about the two made them stand out from all the other passengers who were walking through San Antonio's impressive five-year-old Mission-style Southern Pacific station. Of course, no one knew that the woman's grip contained $11,000 in gold and silver or that she had $50,000 in bills stuffed under her blouse. That was a lot of money in 1907. Adjusted for inflation, the $61,000 in her possession would have the purchasing power of $1.7 million today.

Soon, the pair rented a horse and buggy from a nearby livery stable, and with the gentlemen handling the reins, they drove east from town five or six miles until they reached Salado Creek, a pecan tree–lined stream that flowed into the San Antonio River. "Let's take a bath in the stream," the woman told him, or so he later claimed. They rolled along the bank until they reached a grassy, inviting clearing. There the man hitched the team, and they walked to the edge of the creek. By "take a bath" the lady had meant they should sit on the bank and dangle their shoeless feet in the cool water. It felt good after a long train ride.

Sallie Gibson got off the train intending to buy land and maybe find someone to share her life with. Instead, she nearly found death. *Author's collection.*

Several hours later, a disheveled woman with blood on her head and face, soaking wet, knocked on the door of a nearby farmhouse. In near hysterics, she said that she'd been hit on her head, robbed and thrown into the nearby creek. At first, the residents thought her deranged, perhaps an escapee from a nearby insane asylum. But the woman finally convinced them to call the police.

Detective Charles Van Riper hurried from headquarters to the location. There, Mrs. Sallie A. Gibson, a wealthy widow from Columbia, South Carolina, gave the officer the name and description of the man she said had knocked her out by hitting her on the head with his revolver, pushed her into the water and fled with her money. Clearly, her assailant had not expected her to survive and be able to identify him as thirty-five-year-old Rufus Williams, her erstwhile traveling companion. A family friend, she continued, he had come with her to San Antonio to help her buy ranchland. She told the lawman that she believed he would be catching a train for home as soon as he could and might have already left town.

Van Riper phoned headquarters with a description of the man and asked detective Joe Cassiano to meet him at the Southern Pacific depot, then known as the Sunset Station. The detective needed help because he knew two interstate passenger trains would be leaving San Antonio that evening, the Missouri-Kansas-Texas's *Texas Special*, which went to St. Louis, and the *Sunset Limited*, which went west to Los Angeles and east to New Orleans. After completing the call, Van Riper rushed to a livery stable that was not far from the depot and located the stable boy who had hitched the couple's team earlier that afternoon. The stable employee said he could point the suspect out if he saw him again.

Hurrying back to the depot with the witness in tow, the detective found that the eastbound Southern Pacific train was about to pull out of the station. Van Riper told the conductor to hold the train. Boarding it, he moved down the aisles with the youngster from the stable until he pointed out the man who'd rented the buggy. At his feet was the valise the victim had described. Just as Mrs. Gibson had said, it contained gold and silver coins and a big wad of cash.

Handcuffed and taken to the police station, Williams readily confessed to the robbery and assault, though he did not admit an intention to kill the woman. The only difference between his story and that of the victim was the nature of their relationship. Mrs. Gibson had told Van Riper that Williams was married and had children. He had traveled to San Antonio with her only to assist in her purchase of a ranch and protect her since she carried so much money. They were not lovers. Later, she changed her story a bit and said that Williams had "hypnotized" her into going to Texas.

Williams, however, had a different account of the events that had transpired. He said he'd left his family for Sallie but that guilt had overridden his desire for another woman. "We got to talking about our trip," he said in a written statement, "and [I] told her that I knew I was doing wrong and that I was going back to my wife and children and that she had no business to persuade me to go with her. She said that I was the only one she cared anything for and that she would kill me if I went back." They had more words, he said, but then he got up, found "a stick" and hit her on the head, and she fell into the water. After that, he continued, he took her money and drove back to town. At the livery stable, he dropped off the buggy and team and hired the manager to take him in another buggy to a barbershop. He got a shave and then walked back to the depot and bought a ticket to Atlanta, Georgia.

With Williams behind bars, Van Riper found a boardinghouse where the woman could stay once she got out of the hospital. Then he called it a long but successful day.

The city's two dailies had a field day sensationalizing the robbery, and newspapers all over the nation soon picked up the story. Indeed, the case had all the elements of a compelling news story, though readers were left to speculate whether the robbery and near murder had been the spur-of-the-moment outcome of an unrequited May–December affair or if Williams, intending only to kill the older woman and steal her money, had given her false hope of living happily ever after with him on a sprawling Texas cattle ranch. Despite the fact that newspapers described Mrs. Gibson as "eccentric," "of a nervous disposition," "old" and "plain looking" in the days that followed, she received numerous letters from men proposing to marry her and treat her right. Her wealth surely had no influence on these suitors-by-mail.

Reporters and readers anticipated that the truth about the case would come out at Williams's trial. That proceeding took place in November, but what the prosecution thought would be an easy conviction ended in a hung jury, and the judge declared a mistrial. The state moved to try the case again, but Mrs. Gibson apparently decided it would be too much of an ordeal. She disappeared, and the case was dismissed.

Was Mrs. Gibson truly an eccentric or merely an independent-minded businesswoman with a lot of money in a still male-dominated society? At the time in Texas, women could not even take out a bank loan unless they had a male cosigner. Whatever her personality, Gibson's wealth proved to be more of a curse than a windfall. In February 1913, for the third time since receiving her inheritance, someone tried to rob Gibson by force. This time, it happened in Pine Bluff, Arkansas, where, at some point after her San Antonio experience, Gibson had relocated. Finding that a man had broken into her residence, Mrs. Gibson shot him in the arm. But he grabbed the pistol away from her before she could fire again and began beating her with a board. Still, she managed to fight him off, run outside in her nightgown and scream for help. The intruder escaped but was arrested four hours later.

Only three years later, the *Arkansas Gazette* carried a short notice that Mrs. Sallie A. Gibson, a former resident of Dardanelle, Arkansas, had died on October 12, 1916, in Los Angeles at the age of sixty-three. No details were given, though presumably she went to her grave—wherever that was—still a single, wealthy woman.

The Alamo City caper had been mostly forgotten until Fred Mosebach wrote a long article about it for the *San Antonio Express*. From the way it's written, it's clear that he'd been one of the reporters who covered the story when it first broke. Having seen it unfold, he knew well how the matter could have ended: "If the plan had been carried out as designed, Sallie Gibson would have gone to a watery grave with only a passing notice in the newspapers of the finding of the body of an unidentified woman in Salado Creek, perhaps attributed to suicide."

23

MASHER SMASHERS

For generations, San Antonio authorities allowed open prostitution in their city, either by pretending it didn't exist or through enforcement of city ordinances. A double standard also existed in the way law enforcement looked on the treatment of sex workers versus the protection afforded "decent women." Though police would respond to reported serious assaults in the red-light district, for all practical purposes, sex workers and madams were on their own unless they kept off-duty officers on the payroll as bouncers. But in the Alamo City, men were well-advised to leave the city's respectable ladies alone. Even looking at a woman in an ungentlemanly way could get a fellow in trouble.

The term "sexual harassment" had not yet been coined, but during the early twentieth century, prior to World War I, there was a term for men who objectified women in public: *masher*. What constituted mashing ranged from ogling and catcalling to unsolicited familiarity and groping. Nationally syndicated advice columnist Betty Vincent wrote that a masher was "just a plain cad." She continued, "The first article in a gentleman's code is to show all respect to ladies. The masher ignores this unwritten law. He forces his attentions on women to whom he is a stranger."

Speaking at a meeting of the Bexar County Prohibition Committee on January 15, 1910, chairman W.P. Coleman lamented the level of licentiousness in the city. Women strolling Alamo Plaza, he said, were the subject of "stares and remarks from 'mashers.'" Not only that, a gambling house operated on the plaza, a cockpit near market square drew large

San Antonio police cracked down on sidewalk idlers who ogled the ladies, but a well-jabbed hatpin often proved more effective in discouraging unwanted attention. *Author's collection.*

crowds and nearby saloons did a brisk business. "These are the shame of San Antonio," he said. "You cannot tell me that it does not result from anything except nonenforcement of the law. We need closer organization as a measure of purification of the city and to keep our women folks from insult. What a shame it was to have a shooting scrape in a cockpit; what a shame it is to have a cockpit and to advertise it in our leading papers!"

Mashing, not to mention other unsavory forms of behavior, had clearly gotten out of hand in San Antonio, then the state's largest city. On September 3, 1910, the *San Antonio Light and Gazette* published a brief tirade attributed only to "Observant Citizen." The anonymous resident wrote: "I notice that the police do not make any attempt to stop the oglers from ogling. Any evening, you can find a bunch of oglers standing on the corners in the downtown district, and some of them are actually fresh." The writer went on to observe that "in many Texas cities, the policemen have instructions to arrest the would-be mashers, but here in San Antonio, they seem to run with a free reign."

Whether due to that piece or for other reasons, a short time later Police Chief Charles Van Riper ordered his officers to arrest "all men and overgrown boys found hanging around the corners 'ogling' the women who pass."

"Chasing Off Mashers," read a headline in the September 9, 1910 edition of the *Austin Statesman*. The article beneath reported that San Antonio police had been instructed to "clear corners of all who annoy women." Already, the newspaper continued, in only one day, police made three arrests, each masher having to pay a ten-dollar fine. But the department had more work ahead. While the news article made Chief Van Riper look chivalrous, an editor in East Texas noted that it was "the San Antonio newspapers [that had] started a crusade against the 'mashers'...of that city." Whatever triggered the crackdown, the *Palestine Daily Herald* (September 12, 1910) continued, "Every town has a few of this class of undesirable citizens, and they should be made to get off the street whenever found."

Two verses from a poem published in Brownsville—the state's southernmost city and home to an army garrison established at the beginning of the Mexican War of 1846–48—could as well have described conditions in San Antonio, where soldiers stationed at Fort Sam Houston crowded the streets:

I once knew a dashing young soldier.
He was twenty-two years and no older,
But the girls, fair and sweet,
That he met on the street,
Would always show him a cold shoulder.

One evening, he met with disaster,
He winked at a girl as he passed her;
Her brother stood nigh,
Caught the wink of his eye,
Now the eye that he winked wears a plaster.

Nationwide, the anti-masher crusade had a following only slightly less zealous than those pushing for Prohibition. How people dealt with the masher menace varied by region. In the South and West, particularly, serious sexual offenders often were lynched before they could go to trial. As the *Victoria Advocate* explained, in the South, "the masher sometimes gets perforated as well as mashed." Meanwhile, the *Laredo Times* commented on the anti-masher crackdown in San Antonio. The Alamo City, the newspaper said, was "making a commendable effort to suppress its dude 'mashers.' If they can't be mashed any other way, the steam roller should be applied to them."

In San Antonio and elsewhere, aggressive mashers had more to worry about than paying a fine if caught making eyes at proper ladies. Women annoyed by mashers had begun to weaponize the foot-long hatpins commonly used to hold down their large, feathery hats that were then in fashion. If the *San Antonio Light* and the rival *Express and Evening News* had started the war on mashers, the *Light* had not always been aghast at oglers. In fact, earlier that year, the newspaper had come out against the hatpin trend.

San Antonians read and gained inspiration for combating mashers from reports out of New York, where, as the *Chicago Record-Herald* put it, "the 'goo-goo eyes' nuisance had become so great in New York that a law-and-order league has been organized for the special purpose of protecting women from insult."

Someone—probably a wiseacre newspaper editor—came up with the idea of handing out buttons "to ladies who desire to wear them for the purpose of letting it be known that they have no desire to flirt." But thanks to Chief Van Riper's crackdown on mashers, not to mention the fact that San Antonio city council members had ignored a short-lived movement to regulate hatpin length and use, the need for a "Do Not Flirt" button never arose.

24

BILLIE'S BLUE BOOK

Born in San Antonio in 1870, banker Jesse D. Oppenheimer saw a lot of change in his ninety-four years. One of those changes involved Texas's transition from the wild and wooly "anything goes" mentality of the Old West to a more staid, law-abiding attitude. It's not that vice went away—it just went underground.

"I remember when San Antonio was the 'widest-open' city of its size," Oppenheimer wrote in a short memoir called *I Remember*, which was published not long after his death in 1964. That civic permissiveness, common in all Texas towns of any size, allowed or ignored saloons, gambling and prostitution. "Open gambling was indulged in at the Silver King, Revolving Light, White Elephant, Jack Harris and other minor resorts," Oppenheimer continued.

Beyond gambling, the Alamo City offered residents and visitors a robust nightlife scene. The better-known places included the Fashion, Jack Harris' Star and the Gray Mule. At those theaters, Oppenheimer wrote, "Girls were engaged to circulate among the audience to induce patrons to buy beer at one dollar per bottle, receiving twenty cents per bottle as a commission."

Elsewhere, women made money in a different way. "The red-light district was on the west side known as 'across the creek' [the San Pedro], where the resorts were situated," the aging banker continued. While offering no details on how he knew the names of some of the "resorts," Oppenheimer proceeded to list them for posterity's sake. There was Lilly Gibson's, Sadie Ray's, Ignacia Cortes's, Ione Palmer's, Mande Campbell's and, on Elm

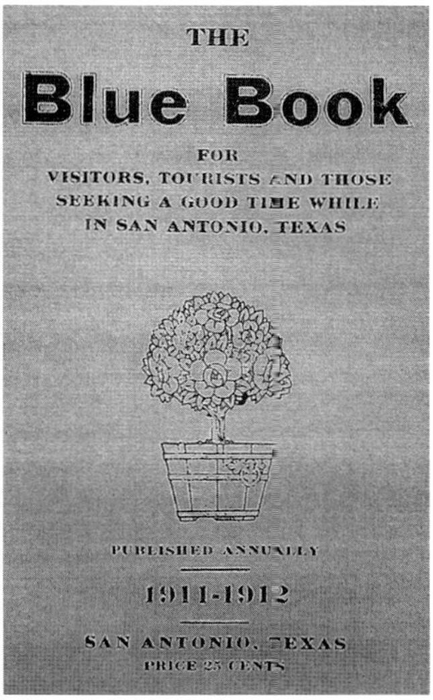

Gentlemen visiting San Antonio could get the rundown on the best bawdy houses in the city's so-called Sporting District by purchasing a copy of this booklet. *Author's collection.*

Street on the east side of town, a place known as Fort Allen. Some of the other houses of ill repute were known only by the digits of their address, as in 101–110, 208, 555 and 777. "During the afternoons, the landladies [better known as madams] would ride in open hacks through the principal streets, each accompanied by several girls all dressed in extravagant fashion," he recalled. Traditional advertising was not necessary.

That's all Oppenheimer had to say about the bawdy side of old San Tone, but there is another publication that illuminates the era of open prostitution in Texas, particularly the Alamo City sex scene. Reprinted in a facsimile edition in the early 1970s, *The Blue Book for Visitors, Tourists and Those Seeking a Good Time While in San Antonio, Texas* initially sold for a quarter. Written by Billie Keilman, proprietor of the Beauty Saloon (not to be confused with a beauty salon) the blue-hued booklet came out annually. The edition later reprinted by Alamo City historian and longtime Bexar County district clerk Elton Cude was originally published in 1911.

The booklet's preface notes that *The Blue Book* was intended as "an accurate guide to those who are seeking a good time." Referring to the booklet, the publisher continued, it would put "the stranger and visitor" on "a proper and safe path as to where he may go and feel secure from 'hold-ups' and any other game usually practiced upon the stranger."

While touting the usefulness of his booklet, Keilman had included a warning printed in large caps: "Do Not Mail This Book." That's because the U.S. Post Office Department back then likely considered the publication illegally naughty, though the preface seeks to address that by noting that any reader "expecting to be regaled with lewd and obscene reading matter will be sadly disappointed, as outside of some harmless wit or toasts, it contains only what necessary information is required to make it a directory." The publisher also noted with obvious pride that *The Blue Book* was only the second such publication of its kind in the U.S., the only other being produced in that noted Louisiana party town, New Orleans.

For decades, San Antonio ranked as the most-populated city in Texas. It also had the largest red-light district. *Postcard from author's collection.*

Filled with advertisements, the twenty-six-page San Antonio booklet breaks the good houses of ill repute into three classes, A, B and C. The "metropolis of Texas" had 24 class A establishments, 20 midrange houses and 62 bottom-rung joints, even though a consumer was supposed to assume that the writer vouched for the safety of all 106 businesses.

The Sporting District, as it was called, extended "south on South Santa Rosa Street for three blocks, beginning at Dolorosa Street, thence from the 100 block to the end of the 500 block on Matamoras Street, thence from the 200 block to the 500 block on South Concho Street and, lastly, the 100 block on Monterey Street." Presumably a newly arrived soldier or visiting conventioneer could pay for feminine companionship elsewhere in town, but the area described in Keilman's booklet was "the boundary within which the women are compelled to live according to law."

For gentlemen interested in the progression from first to third base in a more traditional sense, the booklet listed the San Antonio Texas League baseball schedule.

Though Oppenheimer and other Alamo City old-timers tended to romanticize prostitution, the reality was not always pretty. Four days after Christmas in 1893, the *Light* published a four-paragraph article on the demise of one Frankie Gage, a "disreputable woman" described as being about thirty-five years old. Shortly before sunset on December 29, the newspaper reported, the woman had been seen walking on West Commerce Street "in an apparent happy mood." But a few minutes later, she walked into a residence on Milam Square, "took a large dose of morphine and laid down on the floor to await death." The occupant of the residence phoned police headquarters, and two mounted officers galloped to the scene. Seeing that the woman was in critical condition, they called the city physician, who reached the location within five minutes. But by then, the woman was dead. Coroner E. Griff Jones ruled the death a suicide and ordered her burial at the county poor farm. "Frankie Gage has for a number of years been an inmate of houses of disrepute in this city," the newspaper continued, "and has lived a wretched life. She was broken down and a horrible specimen of humanity, homeless, penniless and friendless."

No matter the form of entertainment offered in the Sporting District, the party finally ended in 1941, when the military threatened to declare downtown off-limits to soldiers if the city did not shut down the brothels.

25

THE AX MAN COMETH

Alfred Louis Casaway, a janitor at the all-Black Grant School, was never late to work, but on the morning of March 22, 1911, he did not show up. That was concerning enough, but for principal H.M. Tarver, it presented a more immediate problem: the janitor had the only set of keys to the school. Tarver phoned attorney R.H. Campbell, whose wife was Casaway's sister, and asked him to see why Casaway had not shown up. The Campbells, the principal knew, lived next door to the Casaways.

Casaway's sister went to her brother's white frame house at 417 North Olive Street and found the front door locked. Knocking and calling out, she received no reply. At that, she went back to her house to summon her husband. He walked over and also called out for Casaway. Getting no answer, he pulled the screen off a back window with the intention of going inside. When he removed the screen, a pillow that had been propped against it fell to the floor, and the attorney saw the fifty-two-year-old Casaway's bloody body lying on his bed. Next to his body was the equally bloody body of three-year-old Louise Casaway, one of his brother-in-law's daughters.

The attorney ran back to his house and called the police. When officers forced their way into the house, they found that all five members of the Casaway family had been murdered, their heads bashed in with the flat side of an ax. The banner headline in that afternoon's *San Antonio Light* summarized the story in only forty-three words:

Family of Five
Murdered in Bed

Louis Casaway, Negro, White Wife
and Their Three Children Victims
of Fiend with an Ax

Bodies Horribly Mutilated

Mother, With Babe in Arms, Found
in One Bed with Heads Beat-
en to Pulp.

Police Have Made No Arrests

Having no idea who slaughtered the family, investigators tried to determine why they had been killed. First, they ruled out robbery or burglary as the motive. Nothing in the house appeared to have been disturbed. Casaway's trousers, containing a gold watch, a few dollars in change and keys to the school, were found hanging from the bedpost. Just as they found nothing to point to intruders bent on taking valuables, in talking with people who knew the family, police learned that Casaway was well regarded among local Black and white residents. In fact, Sheriff John W. Tobin and several of the police officers at the crime scene knew Casaway, who, before taking the job at Grant School, had been a county jailer. He'd also served for a time as a court bailiff.

Originally from New Orleans, Casaway had been an Alamo City resident for more than thirty-five years. He and his wife of ten years were happily married. But Mrs. Casaway was white. Mixed-race marriages were illegal to perform in Texas, so the couple had been married in Mexico.

"Every possible clue is being run down," the *Light* said in a follow-up article the next day. "Every bit of information that might tend to bring to justice the individual, whose bloody deed shocked San Antonio, is not let pass without the closest scrutiny."

A bloody ax that bore strands of brown hair that matched that of Mrs. Casaway was found at the crime scene, but officers were not able to determine if it belonged to Casaway or had been carried to the house by the killer. Officers also found footprints leading away from the house, but they turned up nothing that could tie someone to the murders.

That night, police arrested a man who had reportedly threatened Casaway several years before, but after questioning him, investigators were satisfied that he had nothing to do with the multiple murders and released him.

None of the officers who went to the Casaway house that day would ever forget what they saw, but with no leads to pursue, the case soon went cold and dropped from the headlines. With a revolution underway in Mexico and growing concern that it might lead to war with the United States, the city's newspapers had no shortage of other things to cover.

A year passed, and then it was spring again. Around 7:15 a.m. on April 12, 1912, a young girl knocked on the door of the William Burton residence, a small frame house at 724 Center Street on San Antonio's east side. She had been sent by a neighbor to give Burton a can of oil to replace the oil the neighbor had borrowed the day before. When no one came to the door after she'd knocked several times, Carrie walked to the side of the house and peered in one of the windows. Then she screamed. Running to the house next door, she said Burton was lying on a bed with a knife sticking out of his back. The rest of his family also looked to be dead.

When the first police officer arrived at the scene a few minutes later, he found that all five members of the Burton family had been slaughtered, their bodies bashed and stabbed. The officer telephoned headquarters to report the murders, a call that sent the police chief, Sheriff Tobin and the constable for that precinct rushing to the house with as many officers as they could spare.

The similarities between the Center Street crime scene and the killing of the Casaway family the year before were immediately obvious to the police and the press. "The slaughter of the family," the *Light* reported that afternoon, "similar in every respect to the Casaway crime…and to the recent wholesale slaughter of negro families in Louisiana, is a mystery to the peace officers." Indeed, long before the term *serial murder* entered the vernacular, someone—perhaps several someones—was killing Black families in Louisiana and East Texas. If the two mass murders in San Antonio were connected, they were the westernmost cases. The cases all had similar characteristics: they were perpetrated by someone who entered the homes of Black families in the dead of night, and they were committed by someone wielding an ax. "These circumstances are the same as in the Casaway case," the *Light* continued, "in which it was thought the murder was committed by one crazed on the subject of miscegenation."

As they had the year before, San Antonio investigators quickly ruled out robbery as the motive in the Burton family murders. Nothing in the home

In 1911, someone wielding an ax murdered a Black family of five in this house. A year later, five members of another Black family were killed in the dead of night inside their home by someone swinging an ax. *Author's collection.*

was out of place, and nothing appeared to have been taken. And people who knew the Burtons said the family had no enemies—at least among their acquaintances.

No matter the prevailing racism of the Jim Crow era, San Antonio's newspapers covered the murders thoroughly, and other than noting that the families were Black (which, back then, was routine), they played the story as prominently as they would have had it been a white family. City and county law enforcement come across as equally colorblind in their investigation of the killings. "Sheriff Tobin, Chief [Frank] Newnam, Constable [J.T.] Trainer and every detective is at work on the case," the *Light* noted in its page-one account of the killings.

On April 18, Sheriff Tobin announced a $500 reward was being offered for information leading to the arrest and conviction of whoever killed the Burtons. "I am purposely making the reward higher than usual," Tobin said, "in order to bring to light any evidence that may be in possession of anyone. I will further guarantee them perfect safety and protection from any organization if they will give me the evidence." Two days later, Governor Oscar B. Colquitt offered a $250 reward.

The slaughter of two innocent Black families in San Antonio and the similar murders elsewhere in Texas and Louisiana were disgusting, even to those who still believed Black people were second-class citizens. John S. "K. Lamity" Bonner, the editor and publisher of *K. Lamity's Harpoon*, was often virulently racist in his monthly magazine. "During the last twelve months, a large number of negroes have been brutally murdered by some person or persons in Texas and Louisiana," he noted in the May 1912 issue of his publication. "In every instance, men, women and innocent little children have been brained with an ax as they lay asleep in their homes." While noting that "indications all point to the murderer as being a negro, for an ax is the favorite weapon of the African," he reflected a more enlightened attitude in what he wrote next:

> *No matter whether he be Black or white, I hope* [the killer] *will soon be apprehended and meet with the fate he so richly deserves. Following these brutal murders, many negroes are receiving anonymous threatening letters, evidently written by some hellish white man, which have caused much unnecessary uneasiness among the Blacks. Such an act is the height of brutality, and the writers lay themselves liable to a severe punishment if detected. They ought to be hung.*

The person who really ought to have been hanged was the killer, but his identity was never established.

26

LIKE FATHER, LIKE SON: PART I

Whether future San Antonio City marshal Will Irvin inherited a killer gene or if he was just plain mean is unknowable, but his family history and twenty-first-century scientific research suggest that both factors likely influenced his life—and led to its violent ending.

The oldest of three children, Irvin was born on October 13, 1862, to William H. Irvin Sr. and his wife, Margaret, on his family's stock farm near the long-vanished rural Bexar County community of Cottage Hill. A native of South Carolina, the elder Irwin came to Texas in the 1840s and settled in the Cibolo Creek watershed along the road connecting San Antonio and Gonzales.

When Will Irwin was fourteen, his forty-five-year-old father—acting more like a teenager than a middle-aged man—took insult at not being invited to a shindig that was being planned by neighbors Burrell Lann and Thomas "Tom" Secrest. Irvin sent a note to Secrest challenging him to a fight over the affront. Secrest replied that he'd "see" him in town at the store owned by John Humphrey. On February 21, 1876, Secrest and Lann were inside the store when Irvin rode up. Before Irvin got off his horse, Secrest walked to the front door and, without discussion, let loose both barrels of a shotgun. At about the same moment, Irvin fired one round from his shotgun but missed. Given that he and his horse had just absorbed two fatal loads of buckshot, he hadn't had time to aim. Secrest may have regretted killing a horse, but he disliked Irvin so much that he walked outside just to make sure he was dead. As he bent down to check, someone firing from inside the store put a bullet through his heart, and he fell dead.

Sheriff's deputies arrested James Applewhite, a friend of Irvin's who had been inside the store at the time of the shooting, but a grand jury did not find sufficient evidence to indict him for murder. Clearly, the gunplay had been about more than hurt feelings. Simmering resentments dating from the early days of Reconstruction, amplified by other issues, had ignited one of the many feuds Texas would become noted for. Secrest had been part of one faction, Irvin a part of the opposing faction. That's why no one except the victim found it particularly surprising when, a year later, two men ambushed Secrest partisan John Humphrey, the storeowner. With bullet wounds in his abdomen and wrist, he was taken to his residence, where, before he died, he had time to write a will and tell deputies that he did not know who had shot him. If anyone suspected that Will Irvin and his younger brother James had anything to do with the murder, which certainly seems possible, nothing ever came of it.

For a few years after their father's murder, Will and James helped their mother keep the farm going. In their twenties, the brothers turned to law enforcement. William went to work as a Bexar County sheriff's deputy in 1889, soon joined by James. Both brothers, later hired on with the city as deputy marshals, served as mounted officers and moved up in rank. In 1903, following the election of a new mayor, forty-one-year-old Will Irvin was appointed the San Antonio city marshal. His younger brother continued as a deputy.

Though presumably the department did an adequate job of serving and protecting the residents of Texas's largest city, it does not seem it distinguished itself under Chief Irwin. In the spring of 1904, labor-related violence ranging from rock-throwing to dynamiting got out of hand in the city, and the department did little about it. "What is the matter with San Antonio's police force?" the *Houston Post* asked in an editorial on April 10. On December 13, the Houston newspaper noted, "San Antonio police made a raid and found that gambling has not been suppressed." Eight days later, on orders from Irwin, officers ran Salvation Army solicitors off the street by charging them with obstructing the sidewalk. That, the newspaper reported, would cost roughly a hundred down-on-their-luck folks a Christmas dinner and deprive about fifty families of a holiday gift basket.

When former mayor Bryan Callaghan was reelected after an absence of several years, Irwin submitted his resignation as chief to the Board of Police and Fire Commissioners on June 9, 1905. But Irvin remained on the force as a mounted policeman with the rank of major. His brother would continue as a mounted officer with the rank of captain.

Some indication of the way Irvin had run the department came to light on September 1, when the city attorney filed suit against the former chief

Police headquarters during the time Will Irvin served as chief. *Author's collection.*

to reclaim $250 he had collected in fines and animal pound fees. Irvin had refused to hand over the money. (Elsewhere in the same news article, the amount in question was given as $750.)

By 1909, the police department had stabilized under Chief Charles Van Riper, a highly respected former detective who was so well thought of by his men that they presented him with a diamond pin. A well-run police department helps deter crime, but some offenses are not preventable, especially murder.

Shortly after 4:15 p.m. on Saturday, January 23, someone called police headquarters to report a shooting at 824 South Flores Street. Two horseback officers galloped to the scene, followed by two detectives, Frank M. Newnam and Joe Stowe. When they arrived, the officers saw a Black man lying on the ground behind the residence, groaning in pain. A doctor called to the scene found he had been shot in the abdomen, the bullet penetrating his liver. The victim, identified as Edmond Gabriel, was rushed to the hospital for treatment.

Not long after the shooting, Will Irvin, no longer with the police department, walked into the Bexar County Courthouse office of Constable J.T. Trainer and asked to see him. When told by a clerk that Trainer wasn't in, Irvin told her to get word to the constable that he needed to see him about something important. He said he'd be waiting in Dolan's Saloon, just across the street from the Southern Hotel.

Trainer, meanwhile, learned of the shooting before he returned to his office. When he heard that Irvin wanted to talk to him, he drove to the saloon. Seeing Irwin walking out the front door of the bar, Trainer hurried to him and put his hand on his shoulder. "Will you come with me?" Trainer asked.

"What do you want me for?" Irwin replied.

"You know better than I do," the constable said.

Back at the courthouse, Trainer left Irwin in the custody of two deputies and then drove to the scene of the shooting. There, meeting with city detectives, Trainer told them that he had Irvin in custody. Back at the courthouse, having taken the former chief's .45-caliber revolver, the constable drove Irvin to the county jail and booked him for assault with intent to murder.

Later that afternoon, District Attorney Charles Baker, accompanied by a reporter from the *San Antonio Light*, showed up at the jail. They found Irvin sitting in the office of the chief jailer reading a copy of the afternoon *Light*. Seeing the two, Irvin threw down the paper and stood to shake hands with both.

"What have you done, Will," the DA asked.

"Nothing that I know of," Irvin replied.

"They say you have shot a Negro," Baker said.

"Who? Me? Not me—they have made a mistake. The only thing I shot was a jackrabbit while I was coming to town this morning."

When the *Light* reporter asked Irvin if he'd like to make a statement about the shooting, he declined, saying he knew nothing about it.

From the jail, the state prosecutor went to the city hospital, where, along with a couple of detectives, he took a statement from the gravely wounded victim. Will Irvin had shot him, he said. Later that evening, despite a surgeon's best efforts, Gabriel died on the operating table.

Meanwhile, Irvin remained in custody. On Monday, January 25, Baker presented the evidence in the case to the Bexar County grand jury. Two hours later, the panel indicted the former chief for murder. The defendant was ordered to be held without bail and remained in stir the rest of the week, pending a habeas corpus hearing in which his attorneys would seek his release on bail.

27

LIKE FATHER, LIKE SON: PART II

Knowing they would be seeing legal fireworks, courthouse regulars, friends of the defendant, off-duty law enforcement officers, reporters and curious spectators filled the courtroom when the habeas corpus hearing began on January 30.

The first thing the hearing revealed was the apparent motive in the killing. The month before, at the railroad depot in the small community of Adkins, Irvin waded into a melee involving white, Latino and Black men. While the nature of the fight was not revealed, Irvin tried to defend himself with a heavy piece of wood. As the fighting continued, someone knocked him down and slashed his arm several times with a knife. Testimony revealed that it had been Edmond Gabriel trying to defend himself who had decked Irvin.

The day after the fight, Irvin showed up at the cotton gin where several of those who had been involved worked. This time, he carried a shotgun, not a makeshift club. Over the next several days, he confronted several Black men asking if they had been the one who cut him. All denied it, and Irvin accepted their claims.

Throughout the fall, Irvin apparently kept trying to learn the identity of the man who had cut him. Unwilling to let bygones be bygones, nearly five months later, on January 23, 1909, he was convinced that Edmond Gabriel was the man he was looking for. Learning that Gabriel was a coachman for San Antonio store owner Castanola, he went to Castanola's residence on Flores Street, which is where he found Gabriel. Though Irvin had initially denied shooting Gabriel, at the hearing, his memory seemed to return. Yes, he testified, he had shot Gabriel in self-defense, because he pulled a gun on him. However, no firearm had been found by detectives. But when detectives W.M. Massey and J.D. Nipper went to check again, they discovered a handgun.

The hearing continued until 11:00 a.m. on February 2. Newspapers said it had been the longest habeas corpus proceeding to that point in Bexar County's legal history. The judge ruled for the defense and ordered Irvin released from jail on $10,000 bail. He also ordered a change of venue to Comal County.

On March 11, even the so-called courthouse crowd, the attorneys, reporters and others who spent a lot of time in the red sandstone building, were surprised by the grand jury's action: the body indicted Deputy Sheriffs Massey and Nipper for perjury, a felony punishable with prison time.

Without directly saying so, one of the reporters covering the story did his best to convey what must have seemed obvious to all but the naivest readers:

> *Irvin does not deny having killed* [Gabriel] *but claims to have shot him in self-defense. There were no eyewitnesses to the tragedy,* [but] *no weapon was found on the body of the* [dying man] *when bystanders reached him within a few moments after the shooting, nor was there any trace of a weapon to be found in the vicinity of the tragedy.* [Deputies] *Nipper and Massey, so they testified on oath, later found a pistol…saying they had discovered the weapon in a chicken house about twenty-five feet from where the* [victim] *fell when shot.*

In other words, it looked like the pistol had been planted.

The case was moved to Medina County, where it was tried that spring at the county seat of Hondo. On May 13, a jury acquitted Deputy Massey. A few minutes later, the prosecution moved to dismiss the perjury charge against Nipper. That cleared the way for Irvin's lawyers to proceed with their self-defense case, now that the pistol found at the scene could likely be introduced as evidence.

Irvin went on trial in New Braunfels on September 15 that year. During the four-day proceeding, which newspapers called the most sensational to that point in Comal County history, the prosecution presented thirteen witnesses, while the defense brought sixteen witnesses. One of those defense witnesses was Irvin, who told the jury, "I shot him because my own life was in danger." When the case went to the jury on September 18, the panel was out so long that it looked like they couldn't reach a decision. Finally, at 7:55 p.m., the jury announced it had a verdict—not guilty.

Former chief Irvin's murder trial, moved to New Braunfels in a change of venue, took place in the Comal County Courthouse. *Library of Congress.*

One of the investigators who had testified at Irwin's trial and during the perjury trial that proceeded it was Detective Frank Newnam, an eight-year veteran of the force. On the evening of January 10, 1910, he sat with his wife, Lillie, and their children, eating supper when someone fired both barrels of a double-barreled shotgun at him. "Oh, my God, Lillie, some scoundrel has shot me," he said. The officer was rushed to the hospital, where doctors held little hope for his survival.

Police used bloodhounds to follow the shooter's trail, but the dogs did not pick up anything. The only clue investigators found at the scene was a size 10.5 footprint.

"Within the last few months," one newspaper reported, "[Newnam] has been very active in ridding the city of men who, under the new state law, were termed vagrants. Several well-known characters have served a sentence on the rock pile as a result of his efforts. It is believed they had a hand in the shooting."

Two days later, four Black men were arrested in connection with the shooting. The *San Antonio Light* reported that the district attorney and Police Chief Van Ripper would be taking statements from the four men and predicted the attempted assassination had been solved.

Baker soon began to doubt that the four men in custody had anything to do with the shooting of the detective. By January 15, the prosecutor had not come up with anything that would connect the men to the incident and ordered their release. Meanwhile, doctors announced that Newnam would recover but that he had been blinded in one eye. A $1,000 reward was offered for information that would lead to an arrest in the case. The DA and police chief both still felt that the attempted murder of the detective had been a retaliatory act. The only question was what led to it.

Then, on February 2, a man originally identified as Dan Horner and later identified by the unusual name of Dill F. Sapp was arrested for assault to murder in the Newnam shooting. After that, the DA and the police must have spent a lot of time interviewing the suspect. Assuming the information came from him, on November 29, police arrested former chief Irvin in the shooting of Newnam, who, by this time, had been promoted to first assistant chief of police. The charge was assault with intent to murder.

Irvin quickly posted a $1,000 bond and, through his attorney, waived an examining trial pending grand jury action. On December 16, the grand jury handed down an indictment charging Sapp with assault to murder detective Newnam. But the panel no billed the former police chief. Under Texas and common law, grand jury deliberations are secret, so only the jurors—and perhaps the district attorney and his assistants—ever knew how Irvin had avoided indictment. However, the former chief who was a suspect in an attempted revenge killing, having beaten a murder rap and likely having suborned perjury to support his self-defense claim, did not escape final judgment.

In mid-September 1914, Irvin got into an argument with John Rockowitz, a man who worked on his farm. Rockowitz wanted two dollars a day. Irvin refused to raise his pay, and a quarrel ensued that devolved into a fist fight. The next day, September 18, true to his revenge-minded nature, Irwin showed up on horseback outside Rockowitz's house. With a rifle in his hands, Irvin yelled for Rockowitz to come outside. When Rockowitz did not emerge, Irvin started shooting at the house. At that point, Rockowitz's son, Teofilo, grabbed a double-barreled shotgun and dropped a buckshot shell in each barrel. "As we all were imperiled," the young man later told a sheriff's deputy, "I stepped to an open window to see what could be done. Instantly, a rifle ball struck the sill beside me. I saw Irvin not more than twenty feet away, and I leveled the shotgun at him and pulled both triggers." Unlike Irvin, the younger Rockowitz did not miss. Buckshot ripped into Irvin's face and chest. Falling from his horse, still clutching his rifle, the former chief said, "You have made a good shot!"

The next morning's edition of the *Express* devoted only a nine-paragraph, one-column article to the killing. Appearing on page 18, that edition's last page, the story did not mention the former chief's past criminal charges. Nor did the reporter who wrote the piece allude to what surely some old-timers in San Antonio still remembered—that thirty-six-years before, Irvin's father had also been shot dead off his horse.

28
THE THREE EMMAS

Late in the afternoon on Thursday, November 12, 1914, a distinguished-looking gentleman in a finely tailored suit pulled his horse to a stop and alighted from his buggy in front of a cottage at 532 Hunstock Avenue in the new Laurel Heights subdivision on San Antonio's near south side. The caller was a millionaire several times over and could have easily afforded to be driving an automobile or, for that matter, have a chauffeur take him anywhere he wanted to go. But at fifty-nine years old, German-born Otto Koehler—the wealthy president of the San Antonio Brewing Association (later known as the Pearl Brewery) and Mexican mine owner—had grown up in the horse-and-buggy era, and while forward-thinking in many ways, he still preferred getting around the city the old-fashioned way. Or maybe, even though he was a member of the San Antonio Auto Club, his interest in motor vehicles had soured after his wife, Emma, was badly hurt in a car crash four years before.

Though balding and bespectacled, he was a handsome, fit-looking man with a well-trimmed white mustache. He made sure his horse was securely tied and then walked to the front porch, carrying himself like the confident, successful businessman he was. Koehler knocked on the door, and someone let him in. About fifteen minutes later, around 5:15 p.m., neighbors heard gunshots and screams.

Moments later, Emma Dumpke Daschiel rushed outside the cottage, "screaming at the top of her voice," as one newspaper put it. Bessie Campbell, who lived across the street with her husband, ran from her

Otto Koehler's Pearl Brewery was built in 1894, when the company was known as the San Antonio Brewer's Association. *Author's collection.*

residence to the side of the distraught brunette standing in front of the cottage. Then the two women ran up the steps to go inside. As they did so, they heard two more shots.

Mrs. Campbell hurried down the hall and into the sitting room, where she saw Koehler lying on the floor in a growing pool of blood "breathing his last." If he managed to say anything before he died, it was not reported. Sitting on the floor beside Koehler was Emma Hedda Burgemeister. The tall blond later described by a reporter as a woman "with regular and pleasing features" was bleeding from a "jagged wound" on her left arm. "I shot him to protect myself and my friend," Burgemeister said. And then she went into hysterics.

When the first police officer arrived a short time later, he found a .32-caliber revolver with five empty shells in the cylinder. Also on the floor was a bloody case knife and a .25-caliber semiautomatic handgun that had not been fired. The officer used the telephone in the house to report to headquarters what had happened, and by sundown, the small cottage was full of uniformed officers and detectives, as well as Bexar County sheriff's deputies. Both the police chief and county sheriff were there, along with a contingent of newspaper reporters.

Burgemeister had been placed in the back of the police department's new ten-seater, thirty-horsepower patrol car and rushed to the hospital for treatment for her wound, but Sheriff John Tobin had told her to consider herself under arrest and sent a deputy to guard her room.

The following day, the *San Antonio Light*, *Express* and *Evening News* published banner stories on the murder, while newspapers across the nation carried wire service reports relaying the basic facts of the killing. All the news articles stuck to the classic journalistic formula of answering six basic questions: Who? What? When? Where? How? And why? The first five questions were easy enough, but the "why" would take a while.

Koehler's slaying was also big news in St. Louis, where he had lived before moving to Texas in 1880. His widow was also from the Missouri metropolis, which is where the couple had met and married.

"The authorities today tried to ascertain the relations between Koehler and Miss Burgemeister that prompted him to drive to the cottage where he was killed," the *St. Louis Post-Dispatch* reported in a page-one article the day after the murder. "Immediately after the shooting," the article continued, "it was said she was a trained nurse who had been retained as the constant companion of Mrs. Koehler, who has been in ill health for years. It was said she came to San Antonio from Germany four years ago in company with Mr. and Mrs. Koehler after one of their periodic trips to Europe." But the article continued, "Members of the Koehler family emphatically denied Miss Burgemeister ever had served as a nurse and insisted she was not known at the Koehler home." That said, the newspaper noted, "The cottage where Miss Burgemeister lived is said to have been a part of Koehler's holdings."

Burgemeister told police the same thing she had blurted out to Campbell and Daschiel—that she had shot Koehler in self-defense. But investigators and the physician treating her believed the nurse had cut herself, either so she could claim that Koehler did it or in a suicide attempt. "She [Burgemeister] refuses to make any other statement than the one issued in which she said she killed Koehler to protect herself and her friend," the *Austin American-Statesman* reported on November 15. As the San Antonio correspondent for the *Houston Post* put it in his dispatch, "With…the entire police and detective forces of this city working on the case, the killing of Otto Koehler…is becoming more complicated each hour."

While that was true, to detectives, the newspapers and all but the most ingenuous, it was plain that the killing had all the earmarks of a romantic triangle gone bad: an older man with a lot of money, his ailing wife of thirty-two years and a young, attractive nurse who was hired to take care of the missus and who, after a while, began to see to certain needs of the man as well. As it turned out, what had been going on was more like a love trapezoid.

Twenty-four hours after the shooting, detectives, District Attorney Walter C. Linden and two assistant prosecutors took a statement from Mrs. Daschiel. However, the newspaper continued, "the statement is said to be of such nature that it cannot be given publication." Whatever the woman said, it was sufficient enough for the authorities to arrest her for murder. While perhaps only Burgemeister had pulled the trigger, it was beginning to look to investigators like a conspiracy.

This is because while Burgemeister had been Koehler's mistress, in actuality, she was just the millionaire's most recent mistress. Dashiel had been Mrs. Koehler's first nurse and Mr. Koehler's first mistress. The young nurse's statement has not survived, but she apparently laid all of this out for the detectives and prosecutors. Dashiel said she had ended her affair with Koehler so that she could get married. Still, he let her live in the cottage he had bought for her along with Burgemeister, her replacement both professionally and personally.

As for the late sugar daddy, following embalmment at a local funeral home, Koehler's body was delivered to the three-story stone Koehler mansion at 310 West Ashby Place. Some two thousand people visited the residence to pay their respects, and the following Sunday afternoon, an estimated three thousand people showed up for Koehler's graveside rites. "The funeral cortege was the largest held in San Antonio in many years," the *Houston Post* reported. "More than 150 automobiles, 100 carriages and a large white auto hearse were in the procession." Two of Koehler's friends said a few words, but there were no religious services. The millionaire went to his grave in an expensive bronze casket. Inscribed on it in gold letters was "Otto Koehler 1855–1914."

The murder of such a prominent businessman with so many friends, associates and family members would normally spark outrage, but the last paragraph of the Houston newspaper article was interesting: "Friends of the family have intimated that a prosecution of Miss Emma Burgemeister and Mrs. Emma Daschiel…is not desired and it is probable that the charges will not be pressed." Indeed, Koehler's family seemed strangely willing to forgive and forget. They had given up trying to deny that Koehler had

Beer magnate Otto Koehler and two of his three Emmas, Emma Hedda Burgemeister (*top*) and Emma Dumpke Daschiel (*lower right*). *Author's collection.*

known his killer, but the *Post* reported in another dispatch from the Alamo City that friends of the family were "making efforts to confine the court proceedings to the formality of indictment and dismissal of the case without the introduction of the testimony of the women."

Meanwhile, Koehler's last will and testament was quickly filed for probate. The slain brewer bequeathed all his estate, valued at $3 million (that amount of money would be worth more than $80 million today), to his wife.

On November 19, the DA said his office had found no evidence of conspiracy in the killing of Koehler and dismissed the murder charge against Mrs. Daschiel, whose husband, Martin, had arrived from St. Louis a short time before to arrange for her bail. On November 23, Burgemeister was transferred from the hospital, where she had been under constant guard, to the Bexar County Jail. Three weeks later, on December 15, a Bexar County grand jury indicted Burgemeister for murder. Later that month, her trial was set for February 1, 1915.

Former district attorney and then-current state senator Carlos Bee, representing Burgemeister, tried to get his client released on $5,000 bail, but the DA would only agree to her release if bail was set at $7,500. At a hearing a few days later, District Judge W.S. Anderson sided with the state and set Burgemeister's bond at $7,500. She was released from jail on Christmas Eve.

But on February 1, when the clerk of the court read, "The State of Texas versus Emma Hedda Burgemeister," all were present in Thirty-Seventh District Court and ready for trial, with one exception—the defendant. Senator Bee submitted to the court a letter he had received from his client that she had written on a train headed to New York. She was sailing to Europe, she said, to use her nursing skills to help wounded soldiers in the worsening conflict that would become a world war. Judge Anderson ordered her bond forfeited.

For a woman who had supposedly been so ill as to need a full-time nurse, Mrs. Koehler, as soon as the estate was settled, took control of her late husband's brewing company and other enterprises, which ranged from banking to mining. On Christmas Eve, she deeded eleven acres to the city of San Antonio to be designated as "Otto Koehler Park." If the wealthy widow was upset over her husband's apparent affairs with her nurses, it was not publicly apparent.

Nearly three years after the murder, Burgemeister was back in the United States, albeit no closer to San Antonio than New York City. (Some sources maintain she had never gone to Europe, instead remaining in New York.) From New York, she directed her attorney to file a petition seeking to have her bond forfeiture set aside. Of bigger news was that the motion also said the defendant would be returning to San Antonio to face trial. "She declares that she was coerced and threatened to leave the jurisdiction of the court at the time and implicates several officials and men of prominence in the plot to get her out of the country. She promises to reveal the conspiracy in court," the *Austin American* reported on September 30, 1917. On October 9, the self-proclaimed killer of Otto Koehler returned to the Alamo City from New York.

At a hearing on October 19, Judge Anderson set a new bond at $25,000 and scheduled the trial for January 14, 1919. The principal surety was former Governor T.M. Campbell, her new attorney. But when court convened on the morning of January 14, Judge Anderson continued the trial when the state said a material witness, San Antonio attorney Florence Ramer, had not shown. The judge issued an attachment for Ramer, who was soon located in the North Texas town of Denison, where she had traveled on business, and told to get back to San Antonio.

The trial finally began on Wednesday, January 16. "Two witnesses were examined with slight advantage for the defense," a wire service report summarized. The big day came on January 18, when Governor Campbell put Burgemeister on the stand to testify on her own behalf. Wearing a dark dress, fur hat and muff, with a veil over her face, the defendant swore to tell the truth and nothing but the truth and took the stand.

A native Berliner and trained nurse, Burgemeister said she came to the United States in 1907. Two years later, she moved from New York to San Antonio, hoping a dryer climate would improve her health. In the Alamo City, then a naturalized citizen, she continued working as a nurse. In 1910, she testified, she met and became friends with Emma Dumpke, a nurse who was hired by Koehler to care of his wife. That summer, she continued, Emma Dumpke joined the Koehlers on a trip to Europe. When they returned, Dumpke and Burgemeister roomed together. That's when she learned that her friend and Koehler were having an affair.

And then it got complicated. At some point, Burgemeister also entered into what newspapers later called an "illicit relationship" with Koehler. To facilitate his philandering, Koehler bought the house on Hunstock Avenue and deeded it to both women. In addition, he continued to pay each a monthly stipend.

When Dumpke told Koehler in 1913 that she intended to marry someone in St. Louis, which is where she had lived before moving to Texas, Koehler did not take it well. But Dumpke went ahead with her wedding, which her friend Burgemeister attended. Koehler then turned his attention to Burgemeister, saying he wanted to divorce his wife and marry her. While she said no to that, she apparently continued her liaisons with him. "It was a sordid story which the unfortunate woman had to tell," the *San Antonio Light* reported not so objectively, "but one which held the jury and the courtroom, packed to the utmost with spectators, breathless."

The following day, as the wire services reported, "Rigid cross-examination…by the state" failed to shake Burgermeister's testimony. "I killed him in self-defense," she "declared without emotion." Following her testimony and that of two "minor witnesses," the defense rested.

The state then called Florence Ramer. She said the defendant had come to her office earlier on the day of the killing and that she had been called to the hospital to speak with her client after Burgemeister was admitted. As the Associated Press reported:

> *When the state asked what the defendant had told her upon visiting her office, Mrs. Ramer refused to answer on grounds that it was a confidential communication to a lawyer. This precipitated a clash between attorneys on both sides. The jury was taken from the courtroom, and argument on the point of law regarding admission of this testimony began.*

It did emerge that Burgemeister had gone to Ramer's office to have her prepare a codicil to her will. Left unanswered was why a seemingly healthy thirty-eight-year-old woman felt she needed a will in the first place, let alone why she wanted it changed in some way.

Ramer had testified before the grand jury that indicted Burgemeister, and the state announced its intention to subpoena the grand jurors to reveal what the attorney had told them. But Campbell objected, and Judge Anderson sustained the objection. What the young attorney knew had apparently been the cornerstone of the state's case. Lacking her testimony to whatever it was that she told grand jurors, the prosecution's case was as dead as the late Otto Koehler.

The matter went to the jury at 6:00 p.m. on January 22. At noon the following day, the panel found Burgemeister not guilty. The all-male jury clearly bought the self-defense argument, and based on what is known about the case and what can be theorized, that does seem like the right verdict.

So, why did Koehler go to see Burgemeister that night? The day after Koehler's death, a St. Louis newspaper said Burgemeister had called him to say that she planned to sell the cottage and return to Germany, where her ex-husband was a soldier, and that Koehler had gone to the house hoping to talk her out of it. Or was she trying to blackmail him by threatening to go public about their affair? Or did he go there hoping to finally talk her into marrying him? Or had he gone there for yet another tryst, only to become enraged after being rebuffed? Had he gone there to kill both women? The questions made for a lot of interesting conversations, but Burgemeister had said as much at her trial as would ever be known.

Having seen her name cleared, Burgemeister directed her attorneys to endeavor to recover her forfeited $7,500 bond money. On February 14, they filed a petition with the court of criminal appeals in an effort to reverse the forfeiture. The appeals court dismissed the petition on April 24, but Burgemeister's lawyers kept at it.

A little over a year after her acquittal, on February 11, 1919, in New Orleans, Emma married the man who had been the foreman of the jury that found her not guilty, James M. "Jim" Turley Jr. Afterward, the happy couple settled in at the house where Koehler was killed. For another decade, Emma's attorneys worked to get her forfeited bond money back from Bexar County. Finally, in the spring of 1928, the Texas Supreme Court upheld a judgment in her favor, and Bexar County returned $6,000 to Emma. (The remaining amount had gone toward fees that were paid to the sheriff's office, which were not recoverable.)

After the low-key coverage of Burgemeister's final legal victory, her name disappeared from the newspapers, and how her life went after that is not known. Her husband, assuming they were still married at the time, died at the age of seventy-six on March 30, 1942, and he was buried in San Antonio's Mission Park Cemetery. Twelve years later, on October 29, 1954, the *St. Louis Post-Dispatch* noted that a burial permit had been issued for one Emma Turley, age eighty-two, of St. Louis. If that woman was indeed Emma Hedda Burgemeister, her connection to one of the Alamo City's most sensational murder cases went unreported.

Even less is known concerning what happened to Emma Dumpke Dashier. But the rest of the widow Emma Koehler's life is well documented.

Following her husband's death, she took over management of the San Antonio Brewing Association, kept it economically viable during Prohibition and the Great Depression and lived until 1943 as one of the Alamo City's most respected residents.

The Koehler family continued to brew Pearl Beer until 1969, when they sold the business. The old brewery, a striking nineteenth-century structure on the banks of the San Antonio River, has been restored and converted into an upscale accommodation named after Mrs. Koehler—Hotel Emma. The house specialty at the hotel's bar is a mixture of Pearl Beer, rose cordial, amontillado sherry, botanical gin and grapefruit and lemon juice. They call it "The Three Emmas."

29

THIRTEEN ROPES AT DAWN

If anyone in San Antonio saw the fires or heard all the sawing and hammering that night along Salado Creek next to the army's Camp Travis, they likely dismissed it as "something to do with training."

At the time, the Alamo City was the temporary home of tens of thousands of draftees and volunteers who were being prepared for transport to the front in France as the so-called Great War with Germany continued. But the activity that late night on December 10, 1917, and into the early hours of the following day, had nothing to do with readying soldiers for war. Rather, the army was preparing for another kind of mass death—the secret execution of thirteen Black soldiers convicted of taking part in a race riot in Houston earlier that year on August 23. The riot, which claimed seventeen lives and left twelve people wounded, and its aftermath demonstrated that the border between justice and injustice is thin and easily crossed.

Under cover of darkness, their labors illuminated by bonfires, Army Corps of Engineers troops were building a massive wooden scaffold with two large trapdoors on an eighteen-by-twenty-four-foot platform. The work had to be carried on in secret and completed before dawn. Shortly before 5:30 a.m., the 13 soldiers were awakened, ordered to put on their uniforms and then marched to several waiting trucks. With an escort of 100 infantrymen, 125 cavalrymen, Bexar County sheriff John Tobin and 7 of his deputies, 2 army chaplains and a Black minister from town, the prisoners were driven to the just-completed gallows on Salado Creek.

Black soldiers accused of taking part in a race riot in Houston were tried for mutiny at Fort Sam Houston, and thirteen were hanged in secret. *From Wikipedia.*

The soldiers knew they were about to be executed, but when they saw the gallows, they realized their final request had been ignored. They had asked to die like soldiers in front of a firing squad, not hanged. At least the officer in charge of the execution had ordered that the thirteen unpainted wooden caskets and freshly dug graves be located where the condemned men could not see them.

Their hands cuffed behind them and their feet shackled, the soldiers were lifted out of the trucks and carried up to the scaffold, where they were seated back-to-back in two rows of chairs. Beneath them, the soldiers of Company C, Nineteenth Infantry, stood surrounding the gallows, their weapons at the ready. As other soldiers placed the nooses around their necks, the condemned men began singing religious hymns and bowed their heads for a brief prayer offered by the minister and two chaplains. As the clergymen walked down from the scaffold, the officer in charge shouted, "Attention!" Springing to their feet, apparently having planned their final moments, the thirteen men began singing, "I'm Coming Home." When they finished, they said, "Goodbye boys of Company C."

When his watch showed 7:17 a.m.—the official time of dawn that day—Colonel Millard F. Waltz signaled with the drop of an arm that the trapdoors be sprung, and the soldiers dropped nine feet to a quick death.

After military surgeons confirmed that all the men were dead, the ropes were removed from their necks, and they were placed in plain wooden coffins. Inside each coffin was a sealed glass bottle containing a slip of paper bearing each man's name, rank and date and place of death. As the coffins were lowered into the graves, soldiers were taking down the scaffold and burning the lumber.

"No one approves what the Black soldiers did in Houston," former state representative Maury Maverick and Texas civil rights champion wrote decades later in his weekly newspaper column, "but any person charged with a crime is entitled to due process." But the army paid only lip service to that basic Constitutional right. While trained military and civilian lawyers jointly prosecuted the case, the 118 defendants were represented by only one defense counsel—a man who was not even an attorney. And the military allowed him only ten days to prepare for the trial. Following their conviction in the chapel at Fort Sam Houston, there was no judge advocate review of the proceedings, and no appeal or presidential review was allowed.

Beyond that, the military conducted the execution secretly, with no news coverage until after the fact. The army accomplished this by spreading a rumor that the executions would be held at Camp Stanley, a Fort Sam Houston sub-post thirty miles from town.

Later that year, five additional Black soldiers were hanged at the site of the original mass execution and were buried with the first thirteen soldiers.

The trial of the accused mutinous troops took place in the post chapel, a place of worship given to the army by the people of San Antonio. *Postcard from author's collection.*

A wire fence surrounded the graves, which were marked only with a small metal plaque bearing a number. At the entrance of the small cemetery, the army placed this sign:

> *In this plot of ground*
> *are buried 18 members*
> *of the 24th U.S. Infantry*
> *Hanged near this site for mutiny*
> *At Houston Texas Aug. 23rd 1917*

Over a three-year period beginning in 1934, the remains of eleven of the executed soldiers were exhumed and reburied at Fort Sam Houston National Cemetery, while two other bodies were released to the soldiers' families.

30

A HEARSE FOR JOHN BARLEYCORN

During Prohibition—the time in American history that newspaper editor H.L. Mencken famously referred to simply as "The Horror"—San Antonio gained a new nickname, "Little Chicago." The same was said of other tough towns, including Amarillo and Fort Worth in the Lone Star State, but the Alamo City lived up to its reputation as a violent bootlegging hub. For one thing, it still reigned as the state's most-populated city. But being the first significant Texas city along the main road to Mexico, geography played a larger role in San Antonio's attractiveness to those who smuggled Mexican-made alcohol or manufactured it domestically.

In addition to city, county and state officers, federally commissioned Prohibition agents found no shortage of work in San Antonio. Since "Prohibition agents" can take up a lot of space in a newspaper headline, these lawmen often were simply referred to as "dry agents." One of those dry agents was Charles Stevens, who was killed in a gunfight with bootleggers on the southern outskirts of the city on September 25, 1929.

The Twenties may have roared, but in the early 1930s, Prohibition-related crime continued in San Antonio and elsewhere across the nation.

A seventeen-year-old lineman for the city's electric utility wanted to join the fight, not only in the wet-dry war but against all forms of law-breaking. But he had a problem. You had to be twenty-one years old to join the San Antonio Police Department. A resourceful young man, he grew a mustache, thinking that would make him look older, and easily obtained a poll tax card from a friendly politician who was always looking for votes. A person had to have paid the poll tax to vote, and since you had to be twenty-one to vote, it followed that the possessor of such a card was of legal age. John Klevenhagen, who, despite his desire to seem older than he was, continued to go by Johnny, and was hired as a motorcycle patrolman in 1930. Having grown up on a ranch in adjoining Comal County, he later told an interviewer, "I took to those motorcycles like a duck to the water. Hell, it wasn't much different from riding a raw horse."

As a San Antonio police motorcycle officer, future Texas Ranger Captain John Klevenhagen gave chase to a hearse loaded with bootleg booze. *Author's collection.*

Astride his two-wheeled "horse," a .45-caliber revolver on his hip that he had to pay for out of his own pocket, Patrolman Klevenhagen soon established a reputation as a top-notch, straight-shooting cop—straight-shooting in more ways than one.

On duty one night, not long after he went on the job, he was startled to see a hearse roar past him going way too fast for a city road. He pulled on the road to stop the driver for speeding. Catching up to the vehicle, he saw a shiny coffin through the side window. Thinking the funeral home personnel were sure in the hurry to get to a cemetery, the officer motioned for the driver to pull over. Instead, the driver pressed harder on the accelerator of the somber-looking vehicle. Not only that, the man sitting in the front passenger seat stuck a pistol out the window and opened fire. Klevenhagen braked and then pulled in behind the hearse. Rather than shoot through the back window, Klevenhagen took aim at the vehicle's rear wheels and shot them out. With the driver fighting to maintain control of the vehicle, the hearse swerved off the road and stopped. Gun still drawn, the officer approached the hearse and ordered the passenger to drop his weapon. The man opted to comply. Once he had the two men handcuffed, Klevenhagen, meaning no disrespect to the dearly departed, opened the coffin and found it full of booze bottles.

Despite the gunplay, with no one dead, the arrests hardly amounted to news. If it interested San Antonio reporters at all, the story did not make the wires and only surfaced years later when Klevenhagen—by then a famous Texas Ranger—recalled the incident.

31

THE LITTLE GUN SHOP ON FLORES STREET

One day in June 1933, two well-dressed men in their mid-twenties walked into Hyman Saul Lebman's shop at 111 South Flores Street. Their tailored suits fit in with the shiny black car they'd driven up in, a 1933 Essex Terraplane sedan.

A skilled leather craftsman and saddle maker, the thirty-year-old Lebman had been in business in downtown San Antonio since the early 1920s, selling saddles, harnesses and used guns. He also did repair work, either on leather or firearms. Lebman occasionally paid for a short, classified advertisement to let people know that in addition to selling farm and ranch equipment, he repaired guns. "Mail Orders Invited," one of the advertisements noted. But when you offer a superior product or provide excellent service, word gets around, even if you don't regularly advertise. Considering that the nation was in the middle of a terrible financial depression, Lebman was doing pretty well. And now, two more customers had walked into his shop.

At a glance, Lebman could tell that the men weren't farmers or ranchers. Indeed, they told him they'd recently come into a lot of money in the oil business (no matter that the price of oil had plummeted to only a dime a barrel) and needed a little artillery to protect themselves and their cash. Did he have any machine guns for sale?

A skilled tradesman, Lebman had always enjoyed tinkering with guns, especially the Colt Model 1911 semiautomatic handgun. Adopted by the U.S. Army during the Mexican Revolution and carried by cavalrymen during General John Pershing's punitive expedition into Mexico in search of bandit Pancho Villa, the .45-caliber handgun had become more popular than the old Colt standby, the revolving six-shooter. The Model 1911 held seven powerful rounds, but it fired only one shot when you pulled the trigger. To fire again, you had to pull the trigger again. Tinkering at his workbench, Lebman perfected modifications that could transform the 1911 to a fully automatic weapon. In other words, with Lebman's device, all a shooter had to do was keep their finger pressed down on the trigger, and the weapon would continue to fire until they released the pressure or the clip emptied.

Lebman further modified the handgun with a wooden grip beneath the barrel. That, in addition to the traditional pistol grip, gave stability to the gun when it was fired on full auto. And since his innovation could expend all seven rounds in a matter of seconds, the gunsmith configured his modified 1911s to accommodate eighteen-round clips. For all practical purposes, he had developed a way to turn a semiautomatic pistol into a machine gun. And in the summer of 1933, this was perfectly legal.

Realizing that having military-grade weaponry in the hands of the citizenry might not be the best policy, the Texas legislature passed a law making the possession of an automatic weapon a felony. The measure would go into effect that October. Congress would follow suit the following year with the National Firearms Act, which President Franklin D. Roosevelt hailed as a "New Deal for Crime."

Personable fellows, two self-proclaimed oil barons, Jimmie Williams and Charles Fisher, ponied up the cash for two Colt "super-automatic" pistols and two .38-caliber semiautomatic pistols. Lebman ordered the handguns from a wholesaler in Fort Worth, who shipped them to his shop. There, Lebman transformed them into compact machine guns.

For customers who wanted even better protection, Lebman also sold Thompson machine guns. These weapons, first developed by the army during World War I for use in trench warfare, also fired .45-caliber rounds, but the weapon could accommodate magazines holding up to twenty, thirty or fifty rounds.

In mid-September, Lebman got a letter from Williams ordering more guns. He needed two .38-caliber semiautomatics, two .380-caliber pistols and three .22-caliber rifles. In the same letter, Williams asked if Lebman could get him a Thompson. Lebman replied that he could. The shop owner, fulfilling two separate orders, shipped five Thompsons to Williams in St. Paul, Minnesota, that fall. Lebman usually doubled his money with each sale.

In December, police got a tip that a notorious Chicago gangster named H.L. Keith was in town to see a girlfriend. The informant told investigators where the couple were supposed to meet, and three well-armed city detectives in an unmarked car staked out the place. The officers had not been there long when a taxi pulled up and a woman believed to be the girlfriend walked out of the house and got in.

The officers followed the taxi, but the man in the backseat, despite his preoccupation with the attractive woman sitting next to him, was no amateur when it came to police procedure. Soon realizing he was being tailed, the man believed to be Keith had the cabby pull over, and he jumped out. The three lawmen abandoned their vehicle as well and gave chase on foot. The pursuit went up a dead-end alley at 430 East Commerce Street. As the plainclothes officers ran toward the cornered suspect, he opened fire on them. One officer caught a bullet in the arm. Detective H.C. Perrow was shot in the head and died a few days later. The third officer, still recovering from a hospital stay, fainted, and the suspect escaped.

A short time later, an obviously energized man rushed into Lebman's shop and said he needed to change clothes inside. It was regular customer Jimmie Williams, who had a strange request: Could he borrow a pair of pants? For whatever reason, Lebman did have an extra pair and handed them over to the man. His quick change complete, the man departed as hastily as he'd arrived.

That night, police found out what apartment Keith had been staying in and, with assistance from federal officers, took him into custody. But investigators quickly realized that the man who had mortally wounded Detective Perrow was Lebman's preferred customer Jimmie Williams, not Keith.

The next day, after learning of the incident at Lebman's shop, police took Lebman in for questioning. Seeking to hold him longer, investigators sought a writ of habeas corpus from a state district judge. The state's motion was granted, and police took a lengthy statement from the gun shop owner but did not have enough evidence to charge him with aiding and abetting the murder suspect.

San Antonio police wanted the man who had killed one of their own, but Jimmie Williams was not the most wanted man in the United States. That dubious distinction belonged to John Dillinger, the gangster the FBI had labeled public enemy number one.

Dillinger and his gang were laying low at the Little Bohemia Lodge near Rhinelander, Wisconsin, when FBI agents raided the resort on April 22, 1934. The gang escaped amid a wild shootout, but one of their weapons got left behind. When the bureau traced the serial number of the gun, it found that Wolf and Klar, a firearms wholesale business in Fort Worth, had shipped the gun to Lebman's shop.

Only six days after the Wisconsin shootout, on Saturday, April 28, San Antonio–based FBI special agent in charge Gus Jones and another agent went to Lebman's shop to bring him in for questioning. They grilled him through the night. On Sunday at 7:00 a.m., Jones and another agent went to search the shop. Meanwhile, based on two sworn statements he gave, Lebman was charged in federal court with possessing a stolen government handgun, a Colt Model 1911 that was then in the process of being converted into a machine gun.

First thing Monday morning, Jones called Washington, D.C., to fill FBI director J. Edgar Hoover in on the case. When the SAC told Hoover he believed that Lebman had become a major supplier of machine guns to out-of-state gangsters, the director had a suggestion: share that belief with the press. Exposing the gunsmith might cut into his business. As soon as he got off the phone with Hoover, Jones phoned the city's daily newspapers to tip them to the federal complaint filed against Lebman and added just enough details to give them a sensational story.

With that done, that same day, Jones sent Hoover a four-page, single-spaced letter via air mail and special delivery with much more detail on Lebman and his dealings with known gangsters. In searching Lebman's shop, he wrote, they found some two hundred used rifles and shotguns, fifty used pistols and a dozen new pistols. In addition, the agents found a Thompson submachine gun from which the serial number had been removed. On his workbench, the agents found a Model 1911 that Lebman had been converting into an automatic gun as well as another .45 that turned out to be U.S. Army property. "There is no doubt in my mind but what this man Lebman has been dealing not only with the gangsters mentioned herein but possibly others," Jones continued in his letter to headquarters. Beyond that, the agent said of the defendant, "He is without doubt the biggest liar and unprincipled human that I have ever talked to."

Meanwhile, the *San Antonio Light* and its afternoon rival the *Evening News*, followed by the *Express* the next morning, played right into Jones's hands. "Dillinger's Guns Made in S.A./Gunsmith Is Seized by U.S. Agents," read the headline on the *Light*'s page-one story. "Outlaw Shot Way Out of Trap with Weapon Sold by Dealer in Alamo City," the *Evening News* headline blared. How much the publicity may have impacted Lebman's bottom line is unknowable today, but it didn't make him look good. Despite Dillinger's name being in the headline, there was never any evidence that Lebman ever sold directly to the famed gangster. But he did sell to George "Baby Faced" Nelson, though the gangster used an alias of Lester Gillis.

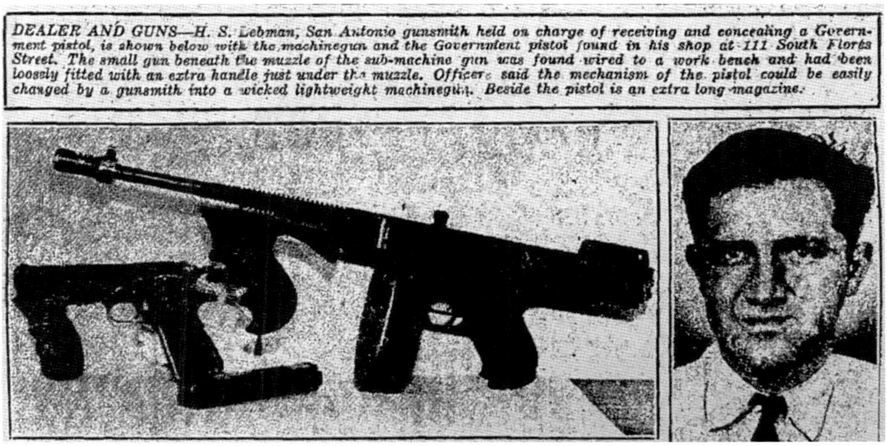

DEALER AND GUNS—H. S. Lebman, San Antonio gunsmith held on charge of receiving and concealing a Government pistol, is shown below with the machinegun and the Government pistol found in his shop at 111 South Flores Street. The small gun beneath the muzzle of the sub-machine gun was found wired to a work bench and had been loosely fitted with an extra handle just under the muzzle. Officers said the mechanism of the pistol could be easily changed by a gunsmith into a wicked lightweight machinegun. Beside the pistol is an extra long magazine.

The Justice Department made sure that the newspapers heard about H.S. Lebman's arrest. This image from the May 1, 1934 issue of the *San Antonio Express* shows the gunsmith and two of his machine guns. *Author's collection.*

As the case against Lebman played out in the courts, on June 8, 1934, the city's two afternoon dailies hit the streets with page-one headlines about the death of a Dillinger gang member, one Tommy Carroll. A killer and a bank robber, Carroll had, the day before, met his Waterloo in Waterloo, Iowa. Cornered by officers who'd been tipped that he might be in town, he reached for his weapon but dropped it when one of the lawmen slugged him. Despite his background as a semiprofessional boxer, Carroll opted to forgo trying to duke it out and hoofed it. That was as far as trying to take him alive went. As he ran, he went down with four bullets in him and died later that day.

San Antonio police had already begun to suspect that the man who'd told Lebman that he was Jimmie Williams was in truth the now-departed Mr. Carroll. Detectives showed a photograph of Carroll to Lebman, who confirmed he was the man who'd changed pants at his shop and one of the men he'd sold machine guns to.

Local and state investigators then focused even more on Lebman's role as a gangster armorer. Soon charged with violation of the 1934 National Firearms Act and the Texas machine gun law, Lebman went on to be convicted on the state charge in August 1935. Though he was sentenced to five years in prison, his conviction was reversed on a technicality. He was tried again, and this time, the proceeding ended in a hung jury.

Lebman ran afoul of federal gun law again in 1970, when he and his two sons, Marvin and Gerald, were named in an eighteen-count federal indictment for illegally selling firearms to individuals from other states but recording the sales as if they had been made locally. Thanks to his lawyers, Lebman never spent a day in prison and only a few days in the local lockup. He continued to operate his gun shop until 1976, when he retired after being diagnosed with Alzheimer's disease. After that, the store no longer sold guns, but the family sold boots, saddles and Western wear until finally closing the shop in 1995, five years after Lebman's death.

Later, Lebman's son Marvin, then a retired attorney, said that his father had sold way more guns to law enforcement officers than he ever did to bad guys. All his dad had done, he said, was sell guns to men in nice suits and hats.

32

THE GATORS OF ELMENDORF

In the fall of 1938, newspaper front pages in San Antonio and across the nation brimmed with worrisome news as a second world war seemed increasingly likely.

How much attention forty-six-year-old Bexar County bar owner Joseph "Joe" D. Ball paid to the building war clouds in Europe is anyone's guess. But Ball did know about war. When the United States entered the so-called Great War in 1917, Ball enlisted in the army and saw frontline combat "over there." Receiving an honorable discharge in 1919, he returned to his hometown of Elmendorf, about fifteen miles south of San Antonio. Ball had made it through the war physically unscathed, but his family and others noticed that when he came home, he seemed like a different person. He drank—a lot. And he never seemed to stay in long relationships with women.

A six-foot-tall rugged-looking man who, in his prime, bore a striking resemblance to the mustachioed Mississippi novelist William Faulkner, Ball did come from a good family. His father, Frank X. Ball, built Elmendorf's first cotton gin shortly after Henry Elmendorf founded the town in 1885. Frank did well as a ginner and later branched out into real estate and retail sales. The Balls were well-to-do, lived in a nice house and were well respected.

The second of Frank and Elizabeth Ball's eight children, Joe Ball grew up like many Texas boys, spending as much time outside as he could, fishing, hunting and prowling the countryside. After he got out of the military, Joe worked for his father for a while but soon quit to make his own way. Like anyone trying to decide what kind of business to enter, Ball wanted to find a product for which there was high demand and low enough supply to justify higher prices. Since national Prohibition had made it much more difficult for a gentleman to enjoy a cold brew or savor a shot of bourbon, Ball opted to become an illicit seller of alcohol—a bootlegger. Soon, Ball was delivering beer and whiskey to his clients with the regularity of a milkman.

While peddling booze was against federal law, for a while, Ball managed to maintain his respected status in the community. After all, he possessed an impeccable pedigree, he'd served his country in a time of war and he minded his own business. In February 1926, when an eight-member Boy Scout troop was organized in Elmendorf, Ball even signed up to be scout master. Three years later, however, Ball got caught disregarding the part of the Scout's Oath that has to do with pledging to stay "morally straight." After being arrested for bootlegging, Ball was convicted in U.S. District Court for violating the National Prohibition Act and was assessed a one-hundred-dollar fine by Judge Duval West.

Ball's name next made the newspaper with a brief notice in the March 4, 1931 *San Antonio Express* that he was planning to get married. While there was no newspaper coverage of Ball's nuptials, three years later, his name showed up in a short, curious article published in the October 8, 1934 edition of the *Express*. Sheriff's deputies had recovered a stolen automobile that was found abandoned near Elmendorf. While that was of little interest to anyone other than the registered owner of the vehicle, deputies were trying to determine why there were bloodstains on the car's seat and running board, as well as blood splatters on the roof. The vehicle had been left on the side of the road near the residence of one Joe Ball of Elmendorf. If investigators ever determined the source of the blood, it was not reported in either of the local dailies.

Six months later, a man suffering from three gunshot wounds showed up at a San Antonio hospital. The nineteen-year-old woman who'd taken him to the emergency room said he'd been shot at Joe Ball's house. She told sheriff's deputies that three armed men had entered the residence and that, moments later, she heard several shots. The intruders then fled in a car. A brief newspaper article about the shooting did not explain why gunmen had shown up at Ball's house or what had been going on there at the time.

The following day, two men were charged with assault with intent to murder in connection with the shooting. The sheriff's department said the shooting had occurred while the victim had been "visiting at the residence of Joe Ball" but offered no further details. Clearly, Ball's place was attracting unsavory characters.

With the end of Prohibition, Ball opened a beer joint in Elmendorf that he called the Sociable Inn. In addition to offering cold beer served by attractive barmaids, Ball built a concrete pool behind his place and stocked it with five alligators. Whether Ball had an affinity for gators or merely saw them as a way to draw customers, the presence of the bumpy-backed reptiles proved good for business, especially at their mealtime. "It was common knowledge that every Saturday night, a drunken orgy occurred around [the alligator pond]," former sheriff's deputy and longtime Bexar County district clerk Elton Cude later recalled. "Any wild animal, possum, cat, dog or any other animal without an owner helped make the show a little better. Get drunk, throw an animal in and watch the alligators....Degrading and degenerate."

In September 1938, a Mexican American man insisting on anonymity for fear of his life approached Bexar County authorities with a disturbing tale. Again, it involved Joe Ball. By one account, the informant visited the sheriff's office in downtown San Antonio to tell his story. More likely is the other version, which is that he shared his concerns with off-duty sheriff's deputy John Gray when he saw the lawman hunting doves in the Elmendorf area. However the sheriff's department first heard about it, the gist of what the man had to say was that he had heard Joe Ball's sister complaining about a barrel Ball had recently placed behind her barn. It stunk to high heaven and had flies swarming all around it. That could have easily been dismissed as a family matter, but the other part of what the nervous man had to say could not be ignored. He was pretty sure the barrel held the remains of a woman who had been killed by Joe Ball.

Deputies Gray and Johnny Klevenhagen were assigned to look into the matter. On Saturday, September 24, the two deputies drove to the Sociable Inn to talk to Ball. When he denied having left a barrel at his sister's house, the officers asked if he would go with them to his sister's place. Ball agreed, probably assuming that his sister would join him in denying any knowledge of a smelly barrel. But she said her brother had been lying—there had indeed been a terribly odiferous barrel there, but Ball and his handyman had removed it.

Based on that, Klevenhagen told Ball he was under arrest for suspicion of murder. Ball asked if they could return to his tavern so he could close it up. Klevenhagen agreed. Back at the tavern, as the deputies looked on, Ball opened the cash register. But instead of gathering up coins and cash, the bar owner grabbed his .45 semiautomatic. Seeing the gun, Klevenhagen yelled "Don't!" as he and his partner went for their guns. If Ball gave any thought to killing the two lawmen and fleeing to Mexico, he changed his mind. Quickly cocking the weapon, he pointed it at his heart, pulled the trigger and crumpled to the floor, dying.

As soon as they could clear the scene, the deputies took thirty-two-year-old Clifton Wheeler into custody. The young Black man had worked for Ball since his bootlegging days. In his interview at the sheriff's office, Wheeler said Ball tended to fall in love—or lust—with the women he hired as barmaids. The first employee Wheeler knew Ball had bedded was Minnie Gotthardt. That relationship went back to 1934, he said. The other two women in the bar owner's life were Dolores "Buddy" Goodwin, a twenty-two-year-old barmaid Ball ended up marrying, and the most recent of Ball's lovers, Hazel "Shotzie" Brown, another of his waitresses. Wheeler said that Ball had shot her to death out of jealousy after she told him she'd fallen for one of his customers and that she intended to quit her job at the Sociable Inn.

Initially, Ball stuffed her clothed body into a fifty-five-gallon drum and took it to his sister's property, where he left the container outside her barn. After she complained about the odor, with assistance from Wheeler, Ball removed Brown's clothing and used an ax to dismember her body. Then they put the remains back in the barrel and took it to a remote area along the nearby San Antonio River. Wheeler agreed to lead the officers to the location, and later that Saturday, the barrel was unearthed and found to contain a female torso and severed limbs. Near the burial site, officers found what little remained of the victim's head, which Ball and Wheeler had tried to burn.

Though the mystery of the foul-smelling barrel had been solved with Wheeler's sworn statement, Ball's hired hand revealed that the case was more complicated than anyone thought. Not only had Ball killed Brown, but the year before, on a lonely beach near Corpus Christi, Wheeler had seen his boss kill Gotthardt. As for the motive, Ball said she had claimed she was pregnant. Telling Wheeler they were going on a fishing trip, Ball took him and Gotthardt to the coast. There, he shot her in the head and, with help from Wheeler, buried her in the sand. With assistance from the Texas Rangers and Corpus Christi–area officers, Klevenhagen and Gray joined in the search for her body. It was recovered after several days of digging.

At first, it was thought Ball had also killed his wife, but Klevenhagen located her in California. Wheeler, meanwhile, was charged with complicity in the murders and convicted, but a jury assessed his sentence at only two years.

As for Ball's five alligators, authorities tied their jaws shut and loaded them into a truck for a one-way ride to the Brackenridge Park Zoo. Some of the Elmendorf alligators were still alive in the late 1970s.

This sensational recap of the Ball case ran in many newspapers across the nation on November 13, 1938 *Author's collection.*

Grisly as the true story was, the Ball case is an interesting study of how rumor, speculation and outright fabrication can transform someone from a philandering, booze-swilling bar owner who killed two women into a mass murder rockstar.

The process began the day after Ball's suicide, when a reporter for the *San Antonio Light* wrote this lead paragraph for his page-one article: "A dramatic suicide, followed by discovery of a nude, dismembered body and a blood-stained ax late Saturday led deputy sheriffs to believe they had a modern 'Bluebeard' in Elmendorf." Anyone who remembered their *Tales of Mother Goose* knew Bluebeard was a folk character from the 1600s who found killing his wives easier than divorcing them. Since then, the Joe Ball story has been told and retold by numerous authors. In the process, in addition to his comparison with Bluebeard, Ball picked up a couple more nicknames, including "The Butcher of Elmendorf" and "The Alligator Man."

Though Bexar County authorities were convinced that Ball had killed only two people, various true crime magazine articles and books on serial killers intimated that his true body count was much higher. Since the development of the internet, websites and publications devoted to serial killers continue to include Ball in their who's who of mass murderers. Some of those sources say the Elmendorf man may have killed as many as twenty women. Conceivably, Ball could have killed that many Germans in France during World War I, but even that seems unlikely. Nor, as some of those online sites maintain, was any evidence ever found that Ball treated his alligators to human flesh.

In the final analysis, Joe Ball was just a bootlegger turned bar owner who, in consuming too much of his brown-bottle inventory, had come to think he could get away with murder. The fact that he just happened to own five alligators was merely a windfall for reporters and true crime writers.

33

MY BLOODY VALENTINE

A Gangland-Style Hit

A handgun is dangerous for more than the obvious reasons. Sure, it can wound or kill. But a pistol can also give a man a false sense of confidence, make him feel that as long as he's packing—even if it's against the law to do so—he's safe.

When the cherubic-faced man got out of his car at 1:20 a.m. that Valentine's Day 1945, he had a piece tucked into his waistband, hidden by his suit coat. And he knew how to use it. Even so, six bullets do no good if trouble arises when you're not expecting it. As he stepped from his car, a shotgun blast sent a load of buckshot in his direction, punching holes in the door of his 1941 Chevrolet convertible. Backpedaling toward the street, he reflexively raised his left arm to shield himself as nine lead balls ripped through the limb and tore into his left side. Still able to stand, he continued to back toward the street when a third load of lead pierced the left side of his chest. Finally, he went down and wouldn't be getting back up, his handgun untouched.

The first uniformed officer to reach the scene at 119 Emory Street on the city's far northwest side near Woodlawn Lake may or may not have recognized the dead man sprawled in a pool of blood on the unpaved caliche driveway near where it met the street's asphalt pavement, but the first detectives on the scene did not have to look at the man's driver's license to identify the victim. It was Hersel H. Gray, the forty-seven-year-old owner of a gambling venue at 213 Broadway called the Studio Club.

WASTE PAPER HELPS VICTORY

SAN ANTONIO

THE LIGHT

AN INDEPENDENT TEXAS NEWSPAPER

HOME EDITION

Member of the Associated Press ★ A Constructive Force in the Community

VOL. LXV—NO. 26 | WEDNESDAY, FEBRUARY 14, 1945 | TWENTY-FOUR PAGES | PRICE FIVE CENTS

Hersel Gray Slain From Ambush by Shotgun Killer

FDR May Tell People Of Parley

The Big Three Conference

The conference which has been held, and apparently concluded, by the leaders of the three great Allied powers is unquestionably of great significance and vital importance to the welfare and peace of the world, now and in the future.

The calling of a United Nations conference in San Francisco in April, for the avowed purpose of preparing the charter of a world peace and security organization, is a project to which all people look with hope.

But what is the moral pattern of the "peace and security" proposed?

If it is in the design of already stricken Poland, who can see reason for hope in it?

It will be a great thing for the world to turn back the German aggression, as will surely be done.

But what will it profit if another aggression is to be rampant and is not to be contested, and is not only to be appeased but even condoned?

If all the people of the world, who earnestly and desperately want peace and security, cannot read the communique of the Big Three conference without misgivings, the fault is with the three powerful men who have decided so much and told so little.

If the American people have fought and sacrificed for a just and good cause in Europe, they are fighting for all this and infinitely more in the Pacific.

Why are the three most powerful men in the Allied world silent about the conflict in which America has its most vital interest, and only willing to announce decisions and perhaps only able to make decisions where the interests of Russia and Britain are paramount?

The American people have the same hopes as the rest of the world in peace and security, and will do all in their power to achieve these worthy things.

But the American people will not mistake a mere show of power by willful leaders for wisdom.

'Red' Berry Booked for Gun-Toting

Canadians, Scots Widen Siegfried Gap in North

Konev Drive Threatens To Split Reich in Two

Rome Rabbi Becomes Catholic

New Commander

Mother Sees Dog Kill Daughter, 2

Congress Gets Voice in Big 3 Agenda

Forecast

World War II got most of the headlines, but a gangland-style hit in the Alamo City was the *Light*'s banner story on February 14, 1945. *Author's collection.*

Suddenly a widow, Mrs. Gray was only able to tell officers that she had heard her husband's car pull into the driveway, followed by the slamming of a car door and three shots in rapid succession. Officers canvassed the neighborhood, but while several residents had heard the gunfire, no one had seen anything.

Not only did Gray have a substantial arrest record in San Antonio and elsewhere, but after two trials, he'd beaten a murder rap in the May 22, 1932 killing of J.A. "Shorty" Mangum in Houston.

Knowing who the dead man was also answered the second fundamental question in any homicide investigation: What was the motive behind the killing? Obviously, the fatal ambush had something to do with illegal gambling. Most likely, someone had decided to literally cut down the competition. Of course, it was possible a love triangle figured into the killing, but that was far less likely.

Unfortunately for police, the answer to the third fundamental question in any murder case was going to be harder to come by: Who did it? Whoever it was he knew not to leave a weapon behind, but they hadn't bothered taking the time to pick up the three empty twelve-gauge shells, 00 buckshot. Nor had the killer thought about the footprints they'd left in the shrubbery where he'd hidden to await Gray's arrival. But in terms of concrete evidence, that was it.

The murder happened too late for the morning *San Antonio Express*, but the apparent gangland hit was the banner headline in the afternoon *News* and its rival, the *Light*.

Homicide detectives led by Sergeant Charles Barrera may have been short of crime scene evidence, but suspicions quickly centered on another well-known local gambler. Less than an hour after the shooting, Bexar County sheriff Owen Kilday and two deputies walked into the Showman's Club in the 500 block of West Commerce Street to talk with its owner, Red Berry. Berry had a pistol on him when the officers descended on the gambling joint, which conveniently enabled them to arrest the forty-six-year-old for carrying a prohibited weapon.

"I think it was a revenge killing, premeditated and coldblooded," the sheriff told a reporter for the *Evening News* later that morning. "I think it could have been the result of recent gambling activities." The sheriff was correct in calling the murder premeditated and coldblooded, but he and his investigators were unable to prove that Berry had anything to do with it. They had witnesses saying that Berry had checked out of the Gunter Hotel at 1:00 a.m., bought three newspapers and arrived at his club between 1:30 and 1:45 a.m. Since the time of Gray's murder had been fixed at 1:26 a.m., it would have been virtually impossible for Berry to drive 3.9 miles from the downtown hotel to what was then the northern suburbs of San Antonio, conceal himself in the bushes outside Gray's residence, kill him and get back to his club, even by the outside estimate of 1:45 a.m. Besides, where was the murder weapon? Officers had not found a shotgun at the club or in Berry's vehicle.

Berry, who later became a member of the Texas legislature, once sponsored a bill to split Texas into two states. In one of those states, he proposed, gambling would be legal. The measure went nowhere, and Berry died in 1969 at the age of seventy. Gray's killing remains unsolved.

34

"DOC" ESTEP AND HIS ATOMOTRONE

Benito Trevino had cancer. His doctor said there was nothing he could do for him other than try to lessen his pain. Desperate, the fifty-nine-year-old San Antonio man consulted three other doctors. All told him the same thing: his condition was terminal.

But then Trevino heard about another doctor who was new to the Alamo City and made an appointment to see him. A bald, heavy-set, affable sort of man, the doctor examined Trevino with a small instrument that seemed to be some kind of meter. Studying the readings, the doctor wrote down a series of numbers on a piece of paper and shook his head. Not only did Trevino have cancer, the clearly concerned physician informed him, but there were issues with his heart as well. This time, however, Trevino heard good news: both his cancer and his heart condition could be cured. All he needed was an Atomotrone, a device the doctor manufactured right there in San Antonio. Trevino was just a working man, not a scientist, but the doctor said his invention was based on his extensive knowledge of nuclear science. The machine enriched tap water with atomic particles, the doctor explained. Once that process was completed, and it didn't take long, Trevino was to drink ten glasses of "E water" a day. "E water," the doctor continued, contained atoms that would break up the cancerous cells that were then multiplying in Trevino's body and flush them from his system when he urinated.

Trevino left that day with renewed hope, eager to tell his thirty-four-year-old son, Ignacio, the good news. The doctor said the lifesaving medical device that he had perfected cost $300 (equivalent to more than $3,000 today), but what did that amount to when compared to being able to live long enough to enjoy his grandchildren?

The younger Trevino, a U.S. Navy veteran, thought it sounded too good to be true. How could something that could be purchased as easily as a television set prolong his father's life? Still, Benito Trevino insisted. Two atomic bombs had ended World War II. Surely, he reasoned, atoms could be harnessed to extend life rather than destroy it. "I couldn't talk him out of it," Trevino later recalled. "He believed in it."

Trevino, a truck driver, drove to the doctor's fashionable Terrell Hills home and reluctantly wrote him a check for the machine on November 1, 1953.

Benito began using the machine as faithfully as he said his prayers. But it didn't work. Instead of getting stronger and gaining weight, Trevino felt worse by the day. And on the day after Christmas that year, Benito Trevino died, leaving behind a wife and three children. His death certificate gave the cause of death as stomach cancer.

Hoping to recover some of his money, Ignacio Trevino sold the machine to someone for $175. It hadn't worked for his father, but the doctor who had prescribed said it could cure anything. Maybe it would help someone else.

As Trevino and his family continued to deal with their grief, on January 12, the *San Antonio Express* published a short article on a hearing that was held the day before at the Bexar County Courthouse. A Mr. and Mrs. William Estep, identified as faith healers, were in court fighting extradition to Illinois, where they faced prison time for violations of the state's Medical Practices Act. Their attorney had succeeded in getting a delay, but the matter was still to be resolved.

After the article appeared, the newspaper began getting phone calls from residents of the Terrell Hills subdivision, one of the city's tonier neighborhoods. Neighbors said people were coming and going from the Estep residence at all hours, often leaving with a large box. Given that Estep was a convicted medical quack, the newspaper's managing editor assigned reporter Charles Ross to start digging into Estep's background to see if he could determine what he was up to in San Antonio. The editor also called Police Chief George Bichsel to ask for the department's cooperation in the investigation. Bichsel called Detective David Keene to his office and put him on the case.

Ross threw himself into the investigation with all the energy of a young reporter sensing a big story. Keene wasn't quite as enthusiastic, but as they began to learn more about Estep and his activities, the detective realized the magnitude of the Michigan native's cruel scam. For one thing, the target of their investigation wasn't even a licensed physician.

Sometimes working ten or twelve hours a day, the two investigators—one with a badge and one with a press card—continued to gather information on Estep. They took sworn statements, made telephone calls across the nation and detailed Estep's activities in San Antonio and elsewhere in Texas. Finally, Ross was almost ready to write a story that would be a classic example of newspaper public service. All they lacked was one of the machines. They weren't making much progress until they received a tip that someone who lived on a certain street had purchased one of Estep's contraptions. Using the latest city directory, they started contacting people who lived on the long thoroughfare. Finally, they found Ignacio Trevino, and he readily told his story. Beyond that, he was willing to let Keene file a theft by fraud charge against Estep. But there was one problem: he no longer had the machine. But with help from the Texas Rangers and law enforcement officers in the Hill Country town of Kerrville, only sixty-five miles from San Antonio, they located the new owner of the machine and were able to seize it as evidence.

This photograph of the Atomotrone was included in a 1964 report by the U.S. Senate Special Committee on Aging, Health Frauds and Quackery. *Author's collection.*

Back in San Antonio, a police radio technician and a private research facility examined the Atomotrone and found it to be nothing more than a mass-produced kitchen cabinet fitted out with a one-watt radio frequency oscillator, a tanning lamp, colored glass and two-gallon-size glass jugs to hold water while it was being enriched with its supposedly curative power. The conclusion of the experts? While everything is made up of atoms, the only thing the Atomotrone was capable of was making illicit money for the man who had designed and manufactured it.

Under a banner headline reading "S.A. 'Healer's' Activities Exposed," the first of a four-part series by Ross ran in *Express*'s January 26, 1954 edition.

A newspaper reporter and a police detective exposed a cruel cancer cure scam artist in the early 1950s, when a lot of people believed the atom could do anything. *Author's collection.*

The reporter's first paragraph got straight to the point: "Old 'Doc' Estep, the Mahatma of 'healers' in the United States, is operating in San Antonio in the exclusive residential section of Terrell Hills."

A con artist of long standing, fifty-eight-year-old "Doc" Estep had been operating in Texas for three years, ever since jumping bond in Chicago following a conspiracy to commit fraud conviction. During their time on the lam in the Lone Star State, Ross reported, Estep and his wife, Dora, had bilked "trusting and unwary Texans" of an estimated $400,000. "His record for fleecing the public, 90 percent of the time with some form of medical activity ["scam" or "con" would have been a better word, but the newspaper's lawyer probably nixed the use of any such noun], dates back to 1923. He always has enough money to stay just one jump ahead of the law."

Indeed, "Doc's" rap sheet—from misdemeanors to felonies—ran for six single-spaced typewritten pages. And now, thanks to the work of Ross and Keene, his record would have one more entry. The night before the first story appeared, an arrest warrant was issued for Estep. Early on January 26, two sheriff's deputies arrested the "doctor" at his residence. Booked in the county jail at 7:00 a.m., he was released at midmorning on $1,500 bond. "This is the foulest fraud I've heard of in my seventeen years on the police force," SAPD Detective Division commander Captain Joe Hester told the newspaper. "It's like tossing a drowning man a short rope."

In the final installment of his series, which ran on January 30, Ross noted that Estep had never used an alias in his scams. "In fact," the reporter wrote, "he's somewhat proud of his thirty-one-year public record and tells each of his customers a little of his background and trouble with the law. He does it in such a way that the 'patient' is led to believe that Estep is a man with a wonderful new invention, being persecuted by the various legal and medical professions."

But "Doc's" past was catching up with him. Ten Texas police departments were looking into his activities within their jurisdiction, the Internal Revenue Service was examining his income tax returns with great interest and just the week before, he'd been indicted on eleven counts of stock fraud. In addition to his long career of making money off desperate, acutely ill "patients," investigators in Dallas found that "Doc" had told several Dallas citizens that he could guarantee them eternal life with a $1,000 infusion of one of his concoctions. After receiving the shot, however, patients did have to check in with him every six months. "Forty thousand people are alive today because of me," Estep told a reporter for Dallas television station WBAP in the summer of 1958 after an appearance before federal judge Thomas W.

Davidson. "I'm an atomic scientist. I invent something that helps people, and they put me in the penitentiary."

Estep's five-year sentence at the Seagoville, Texas federal prison ended up getting reduced for good behavior, and he got out of prison in 1958. Soon, then identifying himself as a bishop of the Kingdom Church of Christ, Estep was back in the Los Angeles area, once again making a living by selling "atomic" healing devices or supposedly nuclear-treated water.

Despite all his legal troubles, Estep never ceased his efforts to bilk the overly trusting. He'd been scamming people since he was a teenager and apparently saw no reason to reform. The last entry in Estep's criminal history was a California conviction for selling bottled water without a license. Still serving time for that, he died at FCI Terminal Island in Los Angeles in February 1967.

35

ROOM 636

Checking into a hotel, even an upscale property, used to be a simple matter. Seldom if ever did the desk clerk ask to see any identification. Usually, all it took to get a room key was cash or check and a signature and address on the guest register. Mr. and Mrs. Smith or Mr. and Mrs. Jones were frequent guests at hotels and motels across the country. That's why the person on duty at the front desk of San Antonio's Gunter Hotel thought nothing of it when he handed the key to room 636 to Albert Knox, a slim man in his thirties who gave a Youngstown, Ohio address. He took the room on February 2, 1965, and was still registered at the downtown hotel six days later.

Some hotel employees later remembered seeing Knox in the company of a petite, attractive blonde, but unless a customer in some way caused trouble, management understood they were renting anonymity along with clean sheets, fresh towels, soap, hotel stationery, a pen and a Gideon Bible.

That's how things stood on the evening of Monday, February 8, when Maria Luisa Guerra, one of the hotel's maids, came to room 636 on her cleaning rounds. It was 5:40 p.m. She later said she hadn't paid any attention to the "Do Not Disturb" card hanging on the door, thinking the room's occupant had merely forgotten to remove it after checking out. But she was wrong; there was still someone in the room.

The maid's innocent intrusion startled Knox, but it terrified the housekeeper. Seeing blood splattered all over the room, she screamed. At that, Knox raised a finger to his lips as if to say "shhhh," grabbed

A man and an attractive woman checked into room 636 at the Gunter Hotel, but only one person checked out. *Postcard from author's collection.*

something wrapped in a large brown paper bag and calmly walked past her. Mrs. Guerra ran from the room to tell another housekeeper, who notified a bellhop who, in turn, summoned the manager. By the time the manager got to the room and decided to call the police, the man who'd been staying in the room had disappeared.

For some reason not explained in the following morning's newspapers, police were not notified until 6:30 p.m. Hotel management surely knew there would be unfavorable publicity when word of what had happened got out, which probably accounts for the delay. Cordially on the part of local media outlets, the initial news articles about the discovery said only the grisly find had been made in a downtown hotel.

The first officers on the scene saw a large amount of blood on the bed, on a chair and in the bathroom. They also found a pair of women's nylon stockings, a pair of men's underwear and a spent .22 cartridge on the bed. "There's little doubt that a murder occurred here," Inspector Joe Hester told reporters. Further, judging from the amount of blood in the bathroom, police believed Knox had dismembered whoever he'd killed. What the killer had not been able to cut up and flush down the commode or otherwise dispose of was probably in that brown bag the maid saw.

"Was a body dissected in S.A. Hotel Room?" the morning *Express* asked in its page-one banner story. Homicide detectives definitely thought so. Assistant Bexar County medical examiner Dr. Ruben Santos quickly determined the blood found in the room was human and told investigators no one could have survived the loss of that much blood. Either a woman's body had been cut up in the room, or it had been the scene of a miscarriage or botched abortion. But the pathologist said he leaned toward the dissection theory.

Police alerted the city sanitation department to be on the lookout for any suspicious packages found downtown and broadcast a pick-up order for Knox, a man who clearly had some explaining to do.

Judging from the bloody footprints found in the bathroom, the woman had small feet. About the only other thing investigators knew about her was that her blood type was A negative and that she liked an occasional stogie. Most people smoked in the mid-1960s, but detectives found several cigar stubs, one of them with lipstick smears. Investigators also found a suitcase containing a new men's shirt, some imported cheese and sardine cans. Four empty wine bottles lay on the floor.

But what the occupants of the room had eaten or smoked did not tell police who they were. Checking with authorities in Ohio, detectives learned the address Knox had given was a vacant lot. And the only person living in

Youngstown named Albert Knox was Black. The man who fled the Gunter was white, and he was clearly not named Knox.

Even though detectives did not have the name of the room's occupant, they had fingerprints. The suitcase the man left behind looked new, and the cheese seemed to have been purchased locally, so detectives started checking downtown stores to see if anyone recalled selling either of the items to a man matching the suspect's description.

Investigators soon located a downtown deli that was the only place in San Antonio that carried the type of cheese found in the bloody hotel room. Even more fortuitously, they found that a local luggage store had sold the suitcase to a man who paid for it with a check for $27.95. The cheese had been purchased with a similar check. Both checks were signed "John J. McCarthy."

When investigators went to the address shown on the checks, they spoke with Mrs. McCarthy, who said she suspected her son of having stolen the checks. He had been living at her home, but he had left on January 27, and she hadn't seen him since. It was after he was gone that she discovered the checks were missing. She had contacted the district attorney's office, and charges had already been filed against her son. His name was Walter A. Emerick, and he was a thirty-eight-year-old unemployed accountant. Mrs. McCarthy said he was a heavy drinker and that when he went on a binge, he often holed up in a hotel.

Emerick had been handled before for check fraud. One conviction netted him probation, but his probation was revoked after he committed another offense, and he'd spent some time in prison. In fact, he'd only gotten out the previous September. Though his criminal history reflected only nonviolent, fraud-related charges, it was beginning to look like he'd graduated to much larger and bloodier things. When the police department's best fingerprint expert compared the prints the department had on file for him with the prints found in the bloody hotel room, they matched.

Based on that, around 8:00 p.m. on Wednesday, February 10, police put out an all-points bulletin that Emerick was wanted as a murder suspect. Lacking a body, investigators still did not have enough evidence to charge him with murder. But detectives sure wanted to ask him some questions. Shortly before the BOLO went out, Sandor Ambrus Jr., the head of security for the St. Anthony Hotel, showed up for work. Soon, he learned that a man who had checked into the hotel the day before had refused maid service and wouldn't open the door when the housekeeper knocked. "I don't want anything," he yelled.

That had not raised any warning flags on the part of hotel management, but Ambrus read the papers and was well aware of what had happened at the Gunter, only two blocks from the St. Anthony. When he checked the registration card the guest had filled out, he saw the man had given the name of Robert Ashley and a Dallas address. A cop at heart, around 11:00 p.m., Ambrus called the police department and told detective Lieutenant George Martin about the guest. Maybe there was nothing to it, but given what Mrs. McCarthy had said about her son's propensity to hide out in hotels, he figured it was worth looking into. The lieutenant went to the St. Anthony and took the card back to the station to compare it with the card the mystery guest at the Gunter had filled out. The handwriting appeared to be the same.

Returning with two other detectives, the lieutenant and Ambrus took the elevator to the fifth floor. The security chief knocked on the door, and they heard someone say, "Who's there?"

"We are police," Detective Frank Castillon said. "We'd like to talk to you." After that, the officers heard a gunshot. Thinking the occupant had fired a shot at them, the men fell back to either side of the door with their weapons drawn. Ambrus put his ear to the door, and when he didn't hear anything, he tried to use a master key to open the door. When the key didn't work, Castillon kicked the door open and burst into the room. There, he found a man in blue boxer shorts and a sleeveless undershirt lying on the bed, a .22-caliber pistol in his right hand. The detective grabbed the gun and tried to get the moaning man to talk, but in a few moments, he was dead.

Identification found on his body bore out what the detectives assumed. The dead man was Emerick. But who had he been with at the Gunter? Detectives had found a woman's cigarette lighter in Emerick's room at the St. Anthony engraved with the initials "C.A.R.," but they never learned her identity, and no remains were ever found.

36

DIAMONDS ARE FOREVER... WELL, MOST OF THE TIME

People from all over the world descended on San Antonio in the summer of 1968 to see HemisFair—a world's fair focused on the two Americas, North and South. This may explain why security guards at the Witte Museum did not ask the short, stocky man in the long-billed cap his reason for walking around the jewelry and rare coin rooms with a green and white aluminum lawn chair in his hands. It could be that those who saw the forty-something man thought he'd brought the chair so he could sit and admire the nationally recognized museum's collection of art and other valuable objects. Still, one woman thought it strange that he seemed to be assessing one of the display cases, tapping the glass and feeling its wood frame as if to judge its sturdiness. The answer to both bits of curious behavior soon became evident.

Just before 4:00 p.m. on Friday, June 4, the man used the two-and-a-half-pound machinist's hammer he'd somehow managed to conceal and smashed open the one-half-inch-thick supposedly shatter-proof glass case holding the world's largest canary diamond, a 49.73-karat precious stone mounted on 18-karat gold, surrounded by a cluster of thirty-one emeralds and seventeen diamonds. Quickly snatching the diamond, the man ran toward the only entrance to the jewelry room. Clearing the door, he wedged the lawn chair he'd been carrying into the doorway in such a way that it would take some time and effort for someone to remove it. Protected from immediate pursuit, the thief ran through the museum and out the back entrance. There, several

Taken from the Witte Museum in 1968 by a smash-and-grab thief, the McFarlin diamond remains missing. *Author's collection.*

witnesses saw him jump into the back seat of a late-model turquoise car, whose driver sped off into the growing rush-hour traffic.

Police rushed to the scene of the spectacular smash-and-grab theft and quickly threw up roadblocks at key intersections across the city. Additional officers descended on the airport. But the thief and his accomplice had disappeared, leaving behind little in the way of evidence—just the abandoned lawn chair, the hammer and one emerald the man had dropped as he ran. Rounding up witnesses, investigators were able to get enough of a description for an artist to make a drawing of the suspect, but the publication of the image and a $5,000 award offered by the Witte brought no results.

While the identity of the thief was a mystery, there was no shortage of information on the history of what he had taken. The diamond had originally belonged to a maharaja of the Maratha kingdom in the Gujarat region of India. Wealthy San Antonio oilman E.B. McFarlin had bought the diamond in New York in 1956 as a gift for his wife, Myrtle. "The Duchess of Windsor was trying to get enough money out of England to buy it," Mrs.

McFarlin later recalled, but her husband beat the duchess to it. Five years later, in October 1961, the McFarlins donated the diamond to the Witte. The museum had the diamond insured for $200,000, but that was $50,000 below its estimated value. Considering the other jewelry taken, the total loss was worth $365,000. Adjusting for inflation, today, that amount would be equivalent to $2.9 million.

Meanwhile, police brought in all the witnesses to view photographs of known jewelry thieves. No one thought any of the photographs were of the man they'd seen at the Witte. Police had been able to lift a fingerprint from the aluminum chair the thief used, but for a fingerprint to do any good, it has to match that of a suspect. On June 24, police interviewed a woman in connection with the caper, but a polygraph examination showed no deception when she denied any involvement in the crime.

The theft received extensive news coverage in San Antonio, across the nation and abroad. While that didn't result in any useful tips, it did stimulate the muse of one local wag who sent a humorous letter to the editor, which was published by the *Express-News* on June 27. "Ever since June 14, I've had this guilt complex," the man began. "I own a two-and-a-half-pound hammer just exactly like the one used by the jewel thief when he busted the…glass and swiped the $365,000 McFarlin diamond." After seeing on television and in the newspapers a photograph of the hammer left at the crime scene, the letter writer said he had hastened to make sure his hammer hadn't been stolen for use in the crime. It was still there, he said, "But still and all, I think maybe I ought to take my hammer down to the police station or somewhere and register it so that I'll be in the clear if the police are looking for people who own two-and-a-half-pound hammers."

However, the writer continued, tongue very much in cheek, that did not mean he favored a strict hammer registration law. But given the jewelry heist, he went on, he could see the need for better hammer control. Such legislation should not restrict the availability of hammers to carpenters or other tradesmen, "but…the sale of hammers through the mail ought to be looked into. You never know what kind of nut you are dealing with when you sell hammers through the mail."

The writer said that some of his friends in the NHA (National Hammer Association) thought controlling the availability of nails might instead be the answer, but he said while that might cut down on the indiscriminate use of the claw hammer, he didn't think it would impact the illicit use of sledgehammers. "I have written my congressman," the writer concluded, "but have not yet received a reply."

The letter—clearly spoofing the nationwide gun control movement that arose following the 1963 assassination of President John F. Kennedy in Dallas—was only the first sign that the apparent inability of police to solve the McFarlin diamond caper struck some San Antonio residents as funny.

That was further borne out by *Express-News* sports editor Dan Cook's coverage of the November 2, 1968 football game between the University of Texas and Southern Methodist University. UT beat SMU handily, despite the best efforts of the SMU quarterback, San Antonio native Chuck Hixon, who had performed under pressure "as cool as the McFarlin diamond trail."

Early the following year, however, the trail grew hot. When Kingsville, Texas police arrested two men for an armed robbery in which a businessman was relieved of $300,000 in rare coins, Texas Ranger Glen Krueger asked one of the suspects, Cecil Yancey Evans, if he knew anything about the Witte Museum diamond theft. Yes, Evans said, he did know something about the stone. He'd been the one who'd stolen it. The answer came so quickly that the Ranger might have thought the suspect was just being cute, but the forty-eight-year-old Galveston man signed a confession, and a Texas Department of Public Safety fingerprint technician matched his print to the print taken from the lawn chair left at the Witte by the thief.

Helpful as that had been, Evans refused to identify the driver of the getaway car. He did tell investigators that after the heist, he had taken the diamond to Phoenix, Arizona, where he sold it for $6,000. Whoever hired him, an individual he also declined to name, had promised to pay $25,000 for the diamond but gave him only $6,000. What became of the diamond after that, the suspect professed he did not know.

Evans served ten years in federal prison for jewelry theft and two years for the coin collection robbery. If he did know where the precious stone ended up after he stole it, that information died with him in 1997.

Diamonds may be forever, but more than half a century after it was stolen from the Witte, the whereabouts of the McFarlin diamond is unknown.

37

"HEY, LET'S HOLD UP THE TRAIN!"

When the masked man holding a pistol approached him, C.A. Berndt thought it was some kind of stunt, perhaps a standing feature of Brackenridge Park's popular miniature train ride—a fake Old West–style holdup. The gunman did seem to be treating the passenger sitting in front of him a little roughly, but no one took it seriously.

When the masked man pushed Berndt down in the seat and held a gun to his head, the fifty-two-year-old Houston man still laughed. But then another masked man appeared and grabbed the purse from Berndt's wife. Finally, it sank in on Berndt and the other passengers that this wasn't part of what they'd paid for. The *Brackenridge Eagle*, a small-scale but realistic-looking engine pulling a long line of open passenger cars with canopy tops, had been stopped by armed robbers.

It happened around 1:00 p.m. on Saturday, July 18, 1970, as the nearly full little train with seventy-five passengers was beginning the eastern segment of its half-hour run. Just as the train came out of a tunnel south of the Witte Museum, two masked men popped out of a stand of thick brush that prevented anyone on nearby Broadway Street from seeing what was happening. Pointing a handgun at twenty-four-year-old engineer Walter Lucas, who had just started working at the park, one of the men shouted for him to stop. He did as he was told. As brazen as stopping the train had been, the two robbers appeared nervous as they walked from car to car, collecting cash and other valuables in a white laundry bag. The bandits quickly disappeared after relieving the occupants of the last car of their valuables, and Lucas used a hand-held two-way radio to call for help.

The nation's last train robbery took place in Breckenridge Park in the summer of 1970. *Postcard from author's collection.*

The train, popular with locals and tourists alike, had been a Brackenridge Park fixture since 1957. A concessionaire paid the city 10 percent of gross receipts for the right to operate the train, which ran along a 3.2-mile, one-fifth-scale track. Initially, the small train was pulled by an engine that looked like a then-modern diesel locomotive, but that engine was later replaced by one that looked like an old-style steam locomotive. They called it *Old No. 99*.

When San Antonio police officers tallied the loss, it came to $500 in cash and other valuables, plus checkbooks, credit cards, car keys and cameras. A felony crime had been committed, but it was still hard to take it seriously. "The Little Train Robbery/Brack Eagle Ambushed—Honest," the *San Antonio Light* headline read the following morning. Beneath the banner were two lengthy news articles giving full details of the incident. The rival *Express-News* played it straighter: "2 Bandits/Rob Train in Park."

Since train robbery is also a federal crime, the FBI joined in the investigation of the holdup. Later that month, the army's Criminal Investigation Division got involved after a tip was received that two soldiers stationed at Fort Sam Houston may have been the robbers. On July 27, officers arrested two twenty-one-year-old soldiers and charged them with the crime. Both were convicted and served time in prison.

A crime is a crime, but some crimes are so unique that they become part of a city's pop culture. That's what happened after the robbery. The *Express*, in a story marking the fifty-year anniversary of the holdup, said that only two-and-a-half years after the robbery, a group of John Jay High School students staged a mock robbery of *Old No. 99* to raise money so a group of local underprivileged kids could go Christmas shopping. When park revenue tanked during the global coronavirus pandemic, the San Antonio Zoo commemorated the fiftieth anniversary of the robbery with a fundraising effort that provided a faux robbery experience for train passengers with each trip it took on the day of the event.

The two young soldiers had made history in a couple of ways. The Breckenridge Park train had never been robbed, and no other train had been robbed in the Southwest since the August 21, 1923 holdup of a Missouri-Kansas-Texas passenger train outside Okesa, Oklahoma. Now, more than half a century has passed since the Little Train Robbery, and its record as the West's last train robbery has held.

38

GEE WHIZ, OFFICER

The visitor had no nefarious intent. He just needed to pee—badly. So, looking around frantically for a place to relieve himself, the man hurried to the nearest bush, hastily went through the necessary preparations and, with an outbreath of relief, let it flow. Unfortunately, a passerby spotted him urinating near the Alamo. Shocked that someone would take a leak outdoors rather than find a restroom, the witness to this most natural and necessary of acts reported the incident to an Alamo ranger, a member of the small security force then employed by the Daughters of the Republic of Texas to protect the so-called shrine of Texas liberty and the park-like grounds around it.

The ranger hurried to the reported crime scene and told the offender to hold it right there, which was exactly what he was doing. But the officer meant to arrest the man for urinating in a public place, a class C misdemeanor punishable by a fine. Panicking at the prospect of a trip to San Antonio's hoosegow, the man tried to run. When the officer, assisted by several San Antonio police officers who had arrived at the scene, corralled the man, he and his colleagues detected a strong odor of alcohol. Not only had the offender gone to the bathroom where there wasn't a bathroom, but he was black-out drunk. Instead of taking him in on a UIPP rap, they booked him for public intoxication.

The prisoner was not some homeless person or a tourist who'd downed one too many margaritas on the nearby San Antonio River Walk. He was the internationally known rock star Ozzy Osbourne, in town for a concert

Police busted rock star Ozzy Osbourne for urinating on the 1939 cenotaph honoring the slain Alamo defenders. *Postcard from author's collection.*

appearance. The only reason he happened to be wearing a dress, he explained, was a music magazine photography shoot for which he'd posed.

From the jail, Osbourne phoned concert promoter Jack Orbin, who came to the lockup and bailed him out for forty dollars—or so he thought. But since the rocker had no memory of his alleged offense, once Osbourne sobered up enough to comprehend anything, Orbin explained that "peeing on the Alamo was like peeing in the queen's cup."

In truth, the rock star had only urinated on the Alamo Cenotaph, a sixty-foot-tall gray marble monument dedicated to the Alamo defenders that was placed in Alamo Plaza in 1939. But to prideful Texans, peeing on the monument was tantamount to peeing on the old mission itself. On further reflection, it occurred to Osbourne that his boozy faux pas had an unseen benefit—he could use it to leverage more publicity. "I've always wanted to piss on the Alamo," he told the packed San Antonio Convention Center audience when he came out on stage. "The White House is next."

If he thought his San Antonio fans would think that was funny, he was wrong. His comment brought a chorus of boos. But accounts that what he said set off a riot were overblown, as was the claim that because of the incident, he had been banned from ever returning to San Antonio. The city council did pass a resolution saying, in effect, that Osbourne shouldn't be invited back, but it did not have the force of law. Still, a decade passed before the now-repentant performer appeared in San Antonio again.

"Ozzy donated $10,000 to the Daughters of the Republic of Texas [which, in 1992, curated the Alamo]," Orbin recalled. "We gave them the money and said Ozzy was a recovering alcoholic. Then-mayor [Nelson] Wolff welcomed him back officially, and we ended up doing two sold-out shows." When presenting his check, Osbourne apologized for the 1982 incident. "We all have done things in our lives that we regret," he said. "I am deeply honored that the people of San Antonio have found it in their hearts to have me back. I hope this donation will show that I have grown up."

Peeing at the Alamo is not the only disrespectful behavior that can end in a person's arrest. In May 2018, a forty-one-year-old man from California was arrested for disorderly conduct and indecent exposure after running naked in front of the old mission while pushing a baby stroller. On another occasion, police arrested a man clad only in his underwear who was riding a stick horse on Alamo property.

Having sex at the Alamo is also a no-no. Two soldiers stationed in San Antonio—a nineteen-year-old man and an eighteen-year-old woman—were taken into custody on an early fall evening in 2004 for copulating on the Alamo grounds. Police filed misdemeanor charges of public lewdness against the couple, who made their own kind of history at the Alamo. In a far more serious case, a forty-three-year-old out-of-state man was handed a life sentence in 2009 for having sex with a fourteen-year-old girl in a men's restroom at the Alamo.

History re-peed itself in 2012.

When a young man wearing a baseball cap walked past an Alamo ranger toward the main entrance of the1700s mission chapel, the officer thought nothing about it at first. But the next time he looked in that direction, the ranger saw that the man had crossed into the chained-off area that is not open to the public. Thinking only to politely ask him to step back, as the guard approached the man, he saw him zipping his pants. Then he noticed an obviously fresh puddle on an area of original mortar. Following procedure, the ranger used his radio to call for a city police officer and detained the man until the officer arrived. When the cop reached the scene, he saw that the visitor had bloodshot eyes and noticed that his breath smelled of alcohol and that he was unsteady on his feet. Given the man's condition and the presence of a pool of urine, the officer arrested the man for public intoxication and urinating in a public place.

The twenty-three-year-old man from El Paso, Texas, sobered up to find that he faced more than a couple of misdemeanor fines. Police had charged him with criminal mischief of a public monument or place of human burial, a felony offense punishable by up to two years in a state jail facility. Then there was the matter of damages. As the arrest report noted, "urine contains salt, and the limestone [of the old mission] absorbs the salt and then pushes the salt out. When the salt gets pushed out, so does the face of the limestone, and through this process, the urine contributes to the eroding of the limestone."

The man pleaded guilty to the criminal mischief charge in exchange for an eighteen-month sentence with no possibility of parole. He also had to pony up $4,000 in restitution to cover the cost of mitigating the damage caused to the façade of the 250-plus-year-old structure.

As one San Antonio reporter got away with saying in print, the visitor from far West Texas had clearly shown "piss-poor judgment" in peeing on the Alamo. But in reporting on the conviction, *TIME* magazine said it best in its headline, "Remember Not to Pee on the Alamo."

BIBLIOGRAPHY

Preface: "The Wickedest City in the Union"

Maverick, Maury, Sr. "We Free a City of Vice and Crime." *Look Magazine*, November 7, 1939.

Panfield, Peter M. *Wild Nights and Roaring Days in Old San Antonio*. San Antonio, TX: Kothmann Publishing Co., 1968.

San Antonio Express. "Sim Hart, 'Cigar Man' in Early Days, Recalls San Antonio of 60 Years Ago; Tells of Killing of Famous Bad Man." January 6, 1932.

San Antonio Light. "Wicked San Antonio/Dixie Williams Says It Is the Wickedest City in the Union." December 7, 1885.

1. CSI San Antonio, 1744

De La Teja, Jesus F. *San Antonio de Bexar: A Community on New Spain's Northern Frontier*. Albuquerque: University of New Mexico, 1995.

Huddleston, Scott. "1700s Lover's Triangle Hinders Today's Alamo." *San Antonio Express-News*, January 18, 2018.

2. Blood-Soaked Sand

Dallas Morning News. "Quinta House Where Patriotic Woman Boxed General's Ears One San Antonio Attraction." January 19, 1936.

Holley, Joe. "At Battle of Medina, Hundreds Died but We Don't Know Where." *Houston Chronicle*, July 13, 2018.

Thonhoff, Robert H. "207th Anniversary of the Battle of Medina, 'The Gettysburg of Texas.'" *Pleasanton Express*, August 12, 2020.

3. Santa Anna's Not-So-Original Sin

Austin Statesman. "The Library Entertainment." November 7, 1875.
Beccerra, Francisco. *A Mexican Sergeant's Recollections of the Alamo & San Jacinto*. As told to John S. Ford. Austin, TX: Jenkins Co., 1980.
Fowler, Will. "All the President's Women: The Wives of General Antonio Lopez de Santa Anna in 19th Century Mexico." *Feminist Review*, no. 79 (2005): 52–68.
Tolbert, Frank X. *An Informal History of Texas*. New York: Harper & Brothers, 1961.

4. Dark Side of the Alamo

Cox, Mike. "Texas Tales." Syndicated newspaper column, March 5, 2008.
———. "Texas Tales." Syndicated newspaper column, May 26, 2004.

5. "I Aim for Your Heart"

Copeland, Cristen Paige. "What Went Wrong? How Arrogant Ignorance and Cultural Misconceptions Turned Deadly at the San Antonio Courthouse, March 19, 1840." Thesis, University of North Texas, May 2008.
Maverick, Mary A. *Memoirs of Mary A. Maverick Arranged by Mary A. Maverick and Her Son Geo. Madison Maverick*. Edited by Rena Maverick Green. San Antonio, TX: Alamo Printing Co., 1921.

6. "Lashes Well Laid On…"

Cude, Elton. *The Free and Wild Dukedom of Bexar*. San Antonio, TX: Privately published, 1978.
Hogan, William Ransom. *The Texas Republic: A Social and Economic History*. Reprinted in 2006. Austin: Texas State Historical Association, 1946.

7. River Nymphs

Everett, Donald E. *San Antonio: The Flavor of Its Past, 1845–1898*. San Antonio, TX: Trinity University Press, 1975.

Frost, John. *Perilous Adventures on Land and Sea*. Chicago: Belford, Clarke & Co., 1888.

Guerra, Mary Ann Noonan. *The San Antonio River*. San Antonio, TX: Alamo Press, 1987.

Mosebach, Fred. "History of City Long Linked to Winding River." *San Antonio Express*, December 31, 1933, 7-C.

8. For Whom the Bell Tolled

Dick, Everett. *The Dixie Frontier: A Social History of the Southern Frontier*. Norman: University of Oklahoma Press, 1991.

Kosub, Allen, and Regina Tolley. "Bexar Slave Patrols." www.losttexasroads.com/history/people/bexar-slave-patrols/.

———. "San Antonio Slave Ordinance." www.losttexasroads.com/history/events/san-antonio-slave-ordinance/.

Miller, Wilbur R., ed. "Slave Patrols." In *The Social History of Crime and Punishment in America: An Encyclopedia*. Thousand Oaks, CA: SAGE Publications, 2014.

Womack, Judy, and Sandra Lee Cleary. *Cibolo, Texas: The Early Years*. Spring Branch, TX: Franklin Scribes Publishers, 2019.

9. Big Henry

Cude, Elton. *The Free and Wild Dukedom of Bexar*. San Antonio, TX: Privately published, 1978.

McDonald, Thomas O. *Texas Rangers, Ranchers, and Realtors: James Hughes Callahan and the Day Family in the Guadalupe River Basin*. Norman: University of Oklahoma Press, 2021.

10. Murdered for a Wagonload of Buffalo Meat

Caldwell, Clifford R., and Ron DeLord. *Eternity at the End of a Rope: Executions, Lynchings and Vigilante Justice in Texas 1819–1923*. Santa Fe, TX: Sandstone Press, 2015.

Cude, Elton. *The Free and Wild Dukedom of Bexar*. San Antonio, TX: Privately published, 1978.

Galveston Daily News. "Hainline Hanged. Another Execution in San Antonio. History of the Crime and the Criminal." August 8, 1879.

11. A No-Account Count or Naive Nobleman?

San Antonio Light. "Count Keroman." February 1, 1882.

———. "An Interview with Count de Keroman/His Version of His Recent Trouble with Dr. Cupples." February 4, 1882.

———. "The Keroman-Cupples Case." February 8, 1882.

———. "The Keroman-Cupples Case." February 16, 1882.

12. The Redemption of William Chrysler

Mosebach, Fred. "Chrysler's Day in Court Recalls His Role of Cadi in Old Bat Cave." *San Antonio Express*, October 27, 1935.

San Antonio Light. "Judge William Chrysler/The Best Man for the Office of City Recorder." February 12, 1887.

13. The Missing Six-Shooter

Cox, Mike. "Texas Tales." Syndicated newspaper column, May 7, 2008.

14. Law and Order at the Alamo

San Antonio Light. "The Haunted Alamo." January 31, 1894.

San Antonio Police Department Historical Society. Post. October 21, 2018. www.facebook.com.

San Antonio Police History Archive. www.sanantoniopolicehistoryarchive.org.

15. Cockfighting

Barber, John. *All the Western States and Territories, From the Alleghanies to the Pacific and from the Lake to the Gulf*. Cincinnati, OH: Howe's Subscription Book Concern, 1867.

San Antonio Express.

San Antonio Light.

16. Mr. Bean, Late of Beanville

Hall, R. Franklin. "Roy Bean Also Flourished Here During Late 70s." *San Antonio Light*, December 31, 1933.

Skiles, Jack. *Judge Roy Bean Country*. Lubbock: Texas Tech University Press, 1996.

17. The Story the Old Sheriff Told

Murphy, Richard. "A Killer with a Hankering for Booze and Brawls, 'Deaf Charley' Hanks Hooked Up with the Wild Bunch." *Wild West*, August 1995.

Stell, Thomas M. "The Killing of Camilla Hanks." *True West*, February–March 1979.

18. "Where Life Is Lively"

Akron (OH) *Daily Democrat*. "Where Life Is Lively/Sports Travel at a Rapid Pace in San Antonio/A Dogberry of the Frontier." October 14, 1893.

Bushick, Frank. *Glamorous Days of Old San Antonio*. San Antonio, TX: Naylor Co., 1940.

Everett, Donald E. *San Antonio Legacy*. Drawings by Jose Cisneros. San Antonio, TX: Trinity University Press, 1979.

19. The Letter of the Law

City of San Antonio. "Codes and Ordinances." www.sanantonio.gov/DSD/Resources/Codes.

Dunphy, Mark. "17 Strange San Antonio Laws You Might Not Know About." *My San Antonio*, December 20, 2019.

20. A Cowboy for to Be

Chicago Inter Ocean. "Harry A. Smith of Busse Ring Leaves Chicago." December 17, 1910. (The newspaper did not say when Smith had left Chicago, only that he was gone. Smith's wife and the mayor said they knew where he was but wouldn't tell the newspaper. If the two Smiths were the same, Smith was already in jail in Texas when this article appeared.)

Galveston Daily News. "Novel Correspondence/How to Become Cowboys by Mail/Six Months in Jail Was Sentence by Court." January 10, 1911.

Palestine (TX) *Daily Herald*. "A Cowboy Factory." December 6, 1910.

San Antonio Light and Gazette. November 20, 1910.

———. "His 'Cowboy Factory' Lands Man in Toils." December 5, 1910.

21. *Adios, Old Gibbet*

San Antonio Light. "Judge Shook Asks Public to View Jail." May 5, 1912.

San Antonio Light and Gazette. "Old Gibbet on Which Ten Men Have Paid Penalty Is Doomed." October 2, 1910.

22. *The Lady and Her Valise*

Austin Statesman. "Offers of Matrimony/Mrs. Sallie Gibson Receives Many Proposals." June 25, 1907.

Dispatch-News (Lexington, SC). "Mistrial in Williams Case." December 4, 1907.

Mosebach, Fred. "Quest for Happiness Blasted as It Is Left on Doorstep at Home." *San Antonio Express*, June 23, 1935.

San Antonio Gazette. "Ten Jurymen Are For Freedom in Williams Case." November 30, 1907.

23. *Masher Smashers*

Austin Statesman. "Chasing Off Mashers/San Antonio Police Given Instructions to Clear Corners of All Who Annoy Women." September 9, 1910.

Fessenden, Marissa. "American Women in the 1900s Called Street Harassers 'Mashers' and Stabbed Them with Hatpins." Smithsonian. October 2, 2015. www.smithsonian.com.

Galveston Daily News. "Johnnies and Johnines." October 3, 1910.

Hix, Lisa. "Masher Menace: When American Women First Confronted Their Sexual Harassers." www.collectorsweekly.com/articles.

Laredo Weekly Times. "Down With the Hat Pin." September 11, 1910.

San Antonio Light and Gazette. "Observant Citizen." September 3, 1910.

———. "Pros Endorse R.W. Hall for Governorship." January 16, 1910.

24. *Billie's Blue Book*

Keilman, William H. *The Blue Book for Tourists and Those Seeking a Good Time While in San Antonio, Texas*. San Antonio, TX: Privately printed, 1911.

San Antonio Daily Light. "A Strange Suicide: A Disreputable Woman Ends an Unhappy Life with Poison." December 30, 1893.

Swartz, Lauren M., and James A. Swartz. *Haunted History of Old San Antonio*. Charleston, SC: The History Press, 2011.

25. The Ax Man Cometh

Bonner, John S., "The Ax Man." *K. Lamity's Harpoon*, May 1912, 18.

Elliott, Todd C., and Peter Levenda. *Axes of Evil: The True Story of the Ax-Man Murders*. Walterville, OR: Trine Day Publishing, 2015.

James, Bill, and Rachel McCarthy James. *The Man from the Train: The Solving of a Century-Old Serial Killer Mystery*. New York: Scribner, 2017.

San Antonio Light. "Family of Five Murdered in Bed." March 22, 1911.

———. "Murder Done by Someone Crazed By Problem of Miscegenation?" March 23, 1911.

———. "Negro Family of Five Slain with Axe as They Slept." April 12, 1912.

26. Like Father, Like Son: Part I

Austin Statesman. "Irvin Held for Killing Negro." February 3, 1909.

Bryan Eagle. "S.F. Sapp Indicted at San Antonio." December 16, 1910.

Dallas Daily Herald. "State News." March 11, 1876.

Houston Post. "A Detective Shot." January 11, 1910.

———. "Two Face Charges." November 29, 1910.

Kosub, Allen, and Regina Tolley. "Cottage Hill." www.losttexasroads.com/history/places/cottage-hill/.

———. "Thomas 'Tom' Secrest." www.losttexasroads.com/history/people/thomas-tom-secrest/.

———. "William H Irvin." www.losttexasroads.com/history/people/irvin-william-h/.

San Antonio Light. "State Fighting Against Giving Bail to Irvin." January 30, 1909.

27. Like Father, Like Son: Part II

Austin American. "Former San Antonio Police Chief Killed by Sayers Station Farmer." September 19, 1914.

Find a Grave. "William Henry Irvin Jr." www.findagrave.com/memorial/53933091/william-henry.irvin.

San Antonio Express. "Former Chief of Police Shot and Killed by Farmer." September 19, 1914.

28. *The Three Emmas*

Austin American. "Rich Brewer's Slayer Refuses to Clear Mystery of Shooting; Sticks to Self Defense Story." November 15, 1914.

Bennett, Steve. "Relaunched Pearl Beer Taps into Its Storied San Antonio Past." *San Antonio Report*, May 17, 2020.

Holley, Joe. "Pearl Brewery Story Is Saga of 3 Emmas." *Houston Chronicle*, November 28, 2014.

Houston Post. "Otto Koehler Buried With Simple Ceremonies." November 16, 1914.

San Antonio Express.

San Antonio Light.

St. Louis Globe-Democrat. "Two Women Held, Accused of Murder of Otto Koehler." November 14, 1914.

St. Louis Post-Dispatch. "Family Denies Knowing Woman Slayer of Koehler." November 13, 1914.

Terraza, Lauren. "'Miss Emma' Saved Her Brewery and Left a Legacy for all of San Antonio." Texas Public Radio, September 12, 2019.

Texas Historical Commission. "Historic Marker Application: Otto Koehler House." Austin, TX, 1988, revised 1989. (A state historical marker was placed on the 1901 vintage Otto Koehler House in 1989. The application says the house, which still stands, is considered "one of the most spectacular examples of turn-of-the-century eclecticism in San Antonio.")

29. *Thirteen Ropes at Dawn*

Haynes, Robert V. *A Night of Violence: The Houston Riot of 1917*. Baton Rouge: Louisiana State University Press, 1976.

Heath, Don. "Solitary Graves Belie Riot's Fury." *San Antonio Express*, December 7, 1975.

Maverick, Maury, Jr. "Carver Details Black Hangings." *San Antonio Express-News*, January 29, 1989.

30. *A Hearse for John Barleycorn*

Meed, Douglas V. *Texas Ranger Johnny Klevenhagen*. Plano: Republic of Texas Press, 2000.

31. The Little Gun Shop on Flores Street

Eger, Chris. "The Lebman 1911 Machine Pistol." September 26, 2012. www.guns.com.

Jones, Gus T. Letter to Director [J. Edgar Hoover], Division of Investigation, U.S. Department of Justice, April 30, 1934.

Lebman (Hyman) v. U.S. Supreme Court. Transcript of record with supporting pleadings, 1972.

San Antonio Evening News. "Outlaw Shot Way Out of Trap with Weapon Sold by Dealer in Alamo City." April 30, 1934.

San Antonio Light. "Dillinger's Guns Made in S.A." April 30, 1934.

Stroud, Scott. "Hidden History of Gangsters and Guns." *San Antonio Express*, November 21, 2010.

32. The Gators of Elmendorf

Cude, Elton. *The Free and Wild Dukedom of Bexar*. San Antonio, TX: Privately published, 1978.

Texas Monthly on Texas True Crime. Austin: University of Texas Press, 2007.

33. My Bloody Valentine: A Gangland-Style Hit

Bird, Chris. "Gambler's Murder Unsolved." *San Antonio Express-News*, February 13, 1995.

Bowser, David. *City of Mystery and Romance: 15 True Stories from San Antonio's Past*. San Antonio, TX: Privately published, 1993.

———. *West of the Creek: Murder, Mayhem and Vice in Old San Antonio*. San Antonio, TX: Maverick Publishing, 2003.

Hersel Henry Gray was born in Fannin County, Texas, on April 17, 1897. At the time of his death, he was married to Cecilia Tettleton Gray (1902–1985). They had one child, Hersel H. Gray Jr. (1926–1982). The murder victim is buried in San Antonio's Mission Burial Park South, Block 7, Lot 450.

34. "Doc" Estep and His Atomotrone

Keene, David. (As told to Howard Hunt). *San Antonio Express*, January 26, 1954.

Kerrville Mountain Sun, "City Police Nab Machine Used In 'Doc' Estep Case." January 28, 1954.

Ross, Charles. "Estep Plans Bared to Expand 'Sales' of Wonder Device." *San Antonio Express*, January 28, 1954.
———. "S.A. 'Healer's' Activities Exposed." *San Antonio Express*, January 26, 1954.
———. "Texas Rangers Enter Probe of Activity of S.A. 'Healer.'" *San Antonio Express*, January 27, 1954.
San Antonio Express. "'Faith Healers' Granted Delay on Extradition." January 12, 1954.

35. Room 636

Cardenas, Leo. "Blonde Is Linked to '636' Mystery." *San Antonio Express*, February 12, 1965.
———. "Room 636 Suspect Ends Life in Another Hotel." *San Antonio Express*, February 11, 1965.
Heath, Don. "Ends Life as Police Close In." *San Antonio Light*, February 11, 1965.

36. Diamonds Are Forever…Well, Most of the Time

Corpus Christi Caller-Times. "Robberies Cleared Up By Suspect." January 10, 1969.
Fort Worth Star-Telegram. "Diamond Theft Appeared Very Ordinary to Witness." June 18, 1968.
———. "New Leads Eyed in Diamond Theft." January 9, 1969.
Mahoney, Noi. "The Case of the Disappearing Diamond and the Disco Duck." www.notorioustxcrimes.com.
Salter, Bill. "Life Term in Coin Theft Case." *San Antonio Express*, February 11, 1969.
San Antonio Light. "$250,000 Diamond Stolen From Witte." June 15, 1968.
Sparkman, Porter. "Witte's McFarlin Diamond Stolen." *San Antonio Express-News*, June 15, 1968.

37. "Hey, Let's Hold Up the Train!"

Allen, Paula. "50 Years Ago, Daring Train Robbery in San Antonio Park Targeted Tourists; Anniversary Recreation to Help Zoo." *San Antonio Express*, July 11, 2020.
Biediger, Shari. "Zoo Train Passengers Relive 'Ambush,' This Time for a Good Cause." *San Antonio Report*, July 18, 2020.

Eaton, Emilie. "Nearly 50 Years Later, Brackenridge Eagle Train Robbery Is Still Famous." *San Antonio Express*, August 23, 2017.

38. Gee Whiz, Officer

Associated Press. "Man Gets 18 Months in Jail for Urinating on Alamo." April 15, 2014.

San Diego Union-Tribune. "Ozzy Osbourne Apologizes For Peeing on the Alamo." November 6, 2015.

Soloman, Dan. "A Brief History of Peeing on the Alamo." *Texas Monthly*, February 5, 2014

ABOUT THE AUTHOR

An elected member of the Texas Institute of Letters, Mike Cox is the author of more than thirty-five nonfiction books. Over an award-winning freelance career dating to his high school days, he has written hundreds of newspaper articles, columns, magazine stories and essays for a wide variety of regional and national publications. When he is not writing, he spends as much time as he can traveling, fishing, hunting and looking for new stories to tell. He lives in the Hill Country village of Wimberley, Texas. Learn more about the author and his work at mikecoxauthor.com.